MANIFESTING MIRACLES AND MONEY

MANIFESTING MIRACLES AND MONEY

How to Achieve Peace, Purpose,
and Plenty Without Getting
in Your Own Way

MICHELLE PAISLEY REED

Published by TCK Publishing
www.TCKPublishing.com

Get discounts and special deals on our best selling books at
www.tckpublishing.com/bookdeals

Sign up for Michelle's free newsletter at
www.WeAreThePowerOf10.com

To my husband, my heart and soul, Jodah Reed.

Without his grounding force and great unconditional Love, I would not be able to reach The Power of 10, and these powerful cutting-edge messages would not be able to come through me to change humanity.

CONTENTS

INTRODUCTION

I was in the middle of a training course on the east coast when something happened that changed the course of my life forever.

I was nervous about performing before a large group of my colleagues. So I meditated, as I often do, in my hotel room. I sat and focused on my breathing. In and out. In and out. In and out ...

And then it happened.

A familiar voice rang out in my mind and clearly said:

"We like to see you succeeding in life."

Now, I've been studying meditation and mysteries of the human mind and deeper connections for years, so I'm quite familiar with hearing "foreign" voices that are not mine. But I understood that this was something entirely different from my inner voice or the spirits I regularly communicate with.

I instantly felt at peace. I felt a warm feeling in my heart, as if I was reconnecting with a long-lost friend. I knew that my life was about to take a whole new turn for the better.

When I relaxed even more and asked who she was (the voice sounded female), they replied that they were "The Power of 10" and that soon I would know more. For now, I should rest.

And then they were gone. I was alone again, but I had this sense of wonderment.

I went on to do quite well in my evaluation, due in part to my increased confidence from listening to this brief encounter.

But when I returned home, the memory of that experience faded away, as most memories do.

A few weeks later, I felt what can only be described as an "urgency" to speak something very important. Thank God my husband is open-minded! I interrupted his work to ask him to please sit with me on our couch, and to allow me to go into a meditative state and record what comes out of me. I was a little scared, as I didn't know what to expect, but I trusted my husband to guide me, and I asked my spirit guides and guardian angels to surround and protect me.

I wiped my mind chatter clean and elevated my vibration as I'm trained to do. I then imagined a large conference room where I took a seat in the back row. I don't remember much of what happened after that, as I went into a deep, full-bodied trance.

When I "came to," my husband had tears in his eyes and was grinning ear to ear. Clearly, what I had said had a profound effect on him. He said, "That was the most beautiful thing I've ever heard. It's going to change humanity." And I believed him.

We were instructed to keep this beautiful wisdom anonymous until the tenth session, so as to spread only the messages of peace and oneness at this time, rather than allow my ego to get in the way. This has never been about me; it's about allowing these voices that come from a non-physical space beyond life and death to come through at a time that our world most needs them.

We were blown away by the response to their messages on social media—thousands of followers within days on Facebook[1], Twitter[2], and Instagram[3].

Within a few weeks, I awoke at 6 a.m. to hear their familiar voice that said, *"Rise and wake up! It's time to write our book."* I've been transcribing their words ever since. It's our sincere hope that combining the written and audio sessions will create a blueprint for moving all of us to a space beyond our current level of understanding.

The transcripts from those first 10 life-changing sessions are included at the end of each chapter, as well as the recordings section of our website at www.WeAreThePowerOf10.com.

Please note: I have chosen to capitalize the words "Love" and "Truth" throughout this book to reflect their higher meaning.

---

[1] http://www.facebook.com/WeAreThePowerOf10
[2] http://www.twitter.com/wearepowerof10
[3] http://www.instagram.com/wearethepowerof10

THE POWER OF 10

Good Morning. Thank you for rising. We have a message which we'd very much like to share with you through the vehicle that is Michelle. She has graciously allowed us to utilize her body for the time being, that we may come through with teachings of peace and oneness, and a place beyond the life and death cycle.

So many of you suffer and learn, suffer and learn, suffer and DON'T learn, so you suffer some more. This is the nature of your choice to return, to advance in karmic cycles, and to keep diving in until you don't need to do it the hard way anymore.

You chose this, and it is not a bad way to go about things. In fact, many souls might find it necessary. It is a starting point, a true adventure for you to learn this way.

And we are here to tell you there is something more; a way out, a way to be which does not require pain.

Are you ready to hear more? Please sit in a quiet pose for a few minutes, or a few millennia, as there is no such thing as linear time. Ask yourself if you can handle a space where there is no more drama. Ask yourself if you'd like to go as high as you possibly can within this framework of a limited lifetime into a dimension that continually expands, where you may manifest at will, where you can finally be truly happy and satisfied and never, ever slip back.

If you feel excited by this process, please continue reading. If not, please hand this book off to a friend.

WHO WE ARE

We are a collective of 10 souls, brought together by our similar frequencies and urgency to teach and advance your planet. We are not aliens, per se, as you will feel us as not so foreign to you, but you in higher form (if you choose). We are non-physical energies who have decided to step beyond the life and death cycle, beyond your ideas of heaven, into the space beyond. And it is GLORIOUS.

Once you have an awareness that this space exists, when you leave the body and graduate into the way station, you will understand that a third option exists where you knew none before.

Let us give you an example: you experience an illness or accident which ends your life story, or you decide to end it yourself. You move into the Light of the way station, which you may envision as a sort of train station, and decide if your story truly is not complete and you need to return to find some sort of "purpose" to your life, or you are enjoying the way station so much you choose to bask in the heavenly lights and heal with the high vibrational entities who reside there. Either is a good and valid choice.

Or, let's say you know of a third option, which you've never seen before. You've never even heard of it because it wasn't part of your story and you weren't ready to graduate yet. Now that you've learned to raise your frequency to an acceptable level, you now see the "train" which is the gateway to higher dimensional levels than you've experienced through countless lifetimes.

This life, you see, is a kindergarten. In kindergarten, you don't understand there is a first grade until the end of the year when your teacher or parent tells you there's something more. And so you finger paint and have fun and concern yourself with learning the rules and making friends and enemies, until it's time to go to the next grade.

Then in first grade, you don't understand there is such a thing as middle school until you reach the end, yes? In middle school, you begin to dream of high school after you are already there and learn of its existence. Toward the end of high school you dream of college and a career and a family ... you get the idea. It is only until you reach a new level of understanding can you achieve the next level of growth.

We are here to tell you that you are almost there.

Most of you, that is. The rest will come along for the ride in time. When you graduate kindergarten, you don't worry much about those who might need to repeat a grade. They will develop when ready. The same is true for you now. Please do not place your focus on those who would bring you down. Their energy is a dense one, and like an egg, you will separate in this process, like a heavy yolk from a lighter egg white.

This does not mean you are not all one. Of course you are! Oneness is all there is, and you must have a basic understanding of this Truth if you are to progress at all. If you find yourself still concerned with the color of your vehicle, of race or gender or culture as a difference, then please hand this book off to someone else.

What this means is that instead of focusing your gaze on those who would do you harm, those who inflict hatred and violence, you look away as you would a child having a tantrum, and HARNESS all your energy to a higher place.

How do you do that?

That is what this book is all about. We wish to teach you various methods of raising your vibration, not only to aid your experience on this dimension, but to assist you in catching that "train" when the time comes—to rise, and rise, and rise, and rise, and to MULTIPLY and AMPLIFY that already existing high vibrational field beyond suffering, to a place where we reside.

Have we said it is glorious?

Q&A - THIS IS ONLY THE BEGINNING

10: Good morning. We are so pleased for you to "use" us. We are The Power of 10, and we are here to greet you. Please, what is your question?

Q: How can we best serve?

A: The question is one of peace and oneness. Your people do not believe. Faith is almost non-existent. What you want is oneness with self and others. But what you have is separation. Our message is one of Truth, of oneness, of peace. Once there is oneness and completeness, there will be no more violence. You must tell the others.

There is a vast circuitry that runs throughout the Universe. You are one small part, very small part. The cosmos is so much vaster than you think. And you are focused on things, and there is so much more.

Q: Why have you chosen Michelle to speak through?

A: This person you know as Michelle is a vehicle. She has clearness and clarity. She must not fight it. We do not wish to take her over, only to be a vehicle for peace and oneness and speech. We come from far away. We no longer have a body. She has a body. She has speech, and she may translate our vibration.

We are beyond the spirits. We no longer reincarnate. It is a choice.

Q: What message do you have for me to deepen my understanding?

A: You must meditate every day. You are on the right path. You are very loving and supportive to Michelle. That is your role. It is not in the words of others. They only point to the Truth. You know the Truth. You must be curious and ask the questions. You are the impetus for her circuitry to be activated. There is more. You have more questions, ask them.

Q: What is the best way to get your message to as many people ...

A: This is only the beginning. The rest will come with patience. We appreciate your enthusiasm. We will all get there with time, as you know it.

We come from a place beyond time. We only wish to help your people to understand a place of peace and harmony that does not currently exist. Your people fight against each other when there is only oneness. Your message is one of oneness. Our message is one of peace.

J: Thank you for showing yourselves to us. I will think of particularly new questions. Please raise her vibration high so that she may channel the spirits she's meant to talk to today. And we'll talk again.

10: The questions they will form themselves, you must not try. Allow them to come from a higher place where they are already.

We are making adjustments to Michelle's body and mind. It will become clearer in the months to come with practice. We thank you for this time. Please encourage Michelle to rest.

One last thing: There is nothing new. Nothing is ever new. It is all recycled. These are only reminders. Only reminders ... It is not time yet to share. This is only the beginning. Thank you.

CHAPTER 1

Wealth

Good morning and thank you for rising. We trust your body received a satisfactory amount of rest?

Please do not be concerned that you did not get up and allow us to write through you at an earlier time. There is no time where we come from—only energy—and so we come to you when your mind is vacant of all else, and most often that is after a substantial period of rest or meditation, which, of course, is your wealth, yes? We'd like to discuss this thing you call "wealth" because it is currently a big focus of yours, and we'd like to clarify its true meaning. Wealth is a state of fullness, a place of being where you feel "filled up" and whole. The Truth is, of course, you already are full from the perspective of Spirit. If you would spend some time each day simply feeling this state of inherent fullness, you would know of no sadness or perceived lack. You say you have no time to do this, but we will remind you that time is a measurement, and it is manmade, as is money.

Money is simply an exchange system created to trade services, drafted on a societal value of each person's worth. You are valuable just because you were born. You started as a thought on another higher dimension, who wished to return to learn lessons and grow your soul, until you reached a place of evolution where you could learn through faith and not suffering. The suffering is part of what you signed up for, but you have a sort of amnesia with this, and you have forgotten, yes? Take time to remember who you were at the way station between lives.

Remember. Yes, you can. We already hear you arguing with us ... just another form of resistance to the Truth of what is. Love is what is. It is the highest frequency and who and what you are made of. Always, throughout all the dimensions. Multiply this feeling you are now experiencing at hearing this times 10, and that's the way you will start to experience the place where we reside. And amplify and expand and multiply AGAIN to 10 x 10 x 10, and ... you get the picture. Isn't that exciting?

Now, when you are alone and true with yourself, you believe when you accumulate a certain amount of wealth you will feel this same level of rampant amplification. But you have it all backwards. AMPLIFY times the Power of 10, and you will feel both full and complete ... happy, on a higher level. THEN, and only then, will you manifest all things toward you, because ironically those things won't matter to you at all anymore.

As you make manifest all the toys and goodies you think will make you happy, you will understand what happens at the way station when you focus your thoughts—only not as rapidly, thank goodness. On the "other side" as you call it, your desires manifest instantaneously because you are not mired down by the density of a body. You can begin to lighten your body-vehicle by lessening the amounts of dense food you feed it and moving it so the cells vibrate in a quicker fashion, but it is only when you release the body that you will know instant manifestation.

And yet, you can come pretty close.

Simply use the word *Rise* each day as you awake and begin your day. The word is a concrete manifestation of energy into form, and so if possible, if you will not wake anyone sleeping next to you, say it out loud with enthusiasm and vigor! Say it 10 times or more, then AMPLIFY, like fireworks. Observe what happens to your level of energy, and note what changes occur throughout your day.

We are NOT saying that manifesting items and things into your world is a "bad" thing at all. In Truth, there is no good or bad—only your perception makes it so. When you reach the way station, many of you will still long for those pleasures you experienced on earth, without experiencing the obstacles and challenges, so it will be a place of great healing. However, when you choose to traject BEYOND life and death, good and bad, to the 10 x 10 x 10 dimensions beyond your ideas of heaven, you will no longer desire those creature comforts, because your alleged void will be filled to overflowing.

Let us be clear: you signed up for this experience and longing while you are here, and so you are simply fulfilling your own destiny and life story you created between lifetimes. And, please know there is so much more to it. You are only getting started.

Just like Love and appreciation and happiness, FREEDOM is who and what you really are. And in your culture and society—in your world, in fact—money equates freedom. Did you ever stop and think that's why you want it so badly? Even those of you who have manifested it from the field of potentiality, and gathered a great deal of it, always seem to want more. It is like a drug, wanting and being addicting to accumulating more of a paper source. And it is so ironic, so silly, given the fact that you already are freedom at the core of your being. Connect with your Source, and you are free. Forever.

Please sit with that for a moment and digest what we just said. Does it resonate with you? Good. You are free, and as you learn you are already free, more and more evidence of this fact will show up in this life story of yours you created. You will also inspire others in your midst that they, too, are already free. And your paper and metal forms of barter will either show up or disappear because you no longer need this to prove your worth.

Over here, we don't use paper or metal to exchange services. We move through our existence enjoying life and teaching others, such as yourselves. We are amused by your early attempts at hoarding money, and even the word *hoarding* has a magnetic resonance—do you feel it? What if you used *giving* and *generosity* instead? Feels much better now, doesn't it?

Think of yourselves as a giant ocean—its waves ebb and flow, ebb and flow, all day long, endlessly. So shall you give and receive, give and receive energy, as a sort of dance, as a melody. Make it so, and it won't seem so tiresome. And we promise, as you do this and raise your frequency and vibration, you will no longer rely on your giant system of trade that you created.

SUFFERING

We would like to share with you our ideas on your suffering. Why you do it, why you encase yourself in it, and how to transcend it.

There are different forms of your suffering, yes? Physical, mental, and emotional. We will go over each and the educational differences. All are contrasting pieces of your true form, which is of course peace.

Physical pain occurs when you resist what is in search of something better, something you believe is better, which bridges the gap into mental. It is stopping the natural flow of the Universe throughout your body as it attempts to create peace and harmony.

Like a dam in a river, it does not feel good to do this. You do it simply to understand that the dam is there, to prove its existence. Once you see it is there, you can simply remove it with your heart, and your body will return to its natural state of health and vitality. Energy always runs through us.

When you focus your mind on the dam instead of the flow, and you curse its existence, you remain dammed up and in pain. It is why you curse each other by stating emphatically, "Damn you!" You just spelled it wrong.

What if you welcomed the damning dam into your awareness? Blessed it for showing you where you might be blocking your own good and the ever-present flow of creative source energy in your body (what many name *prana* or *chi* or life force energy) and observed the many obstacles dissipate? Could you be the witness of this supposed destruction in your body? If you could, you would be the master of your vehicle instead of its victim. Be the beaver, not the dam.

As you learn to do this, perhaps even visualizing the dam to the river in your mind's eye, your spirit will inevitably begin to flow again. All manner of what you call miracles and synchronicities will unfold, as that is the way of our world in each moment. You will catch glimpses of what it means to transcend the life and death cycle, which equates to the faith vs. suffering cycle, and you will know in your heart of hearts that this is what is real, and has been all along.

You may pray to entities that help you with this, but the power is already in you, the same as it is in them, and equally as strong. You personify them as if they were still in human form, and therefore not as schooled in the process. They are neither ahead or behind you, as that is still linear thinking. Yet we do not recommend you beating yourself up over thinking in rising lines, as that is part of what you signed up for in this grand adventure ride you signed up for. Take out the lines, and there you have it: Rise. Rise, rise, rise and you won't justify the need for any sort of process whatsoever. Use the words themselves as tools to make manifest the energy within you. When you pray, see your chosen entities beside you and supporting you in this process, as they all are, and so are we. We are here to watch you progress and grow. As we told Michelle at the beginning of her awakening, "We like to see you succeeding."

So as you see, suffering is entirely unnecessary and overrated, after you've learned your "hard" lessons that you signed up for. Once you are done doing things the difficult way, once you are done telling yourself that enlightenment is "hard work," you will bubble up to new ways of being in your world which will make it that much easier to switch trains once you reach the way station. Be the bubble instead of the mule.

LOVE

How do you do this, you ask? How do you switch trains and feel your "bubbleness"? To merge with the reality of your nature, you must FEEL Love. And to understand what Love is, you must learn to Love another and see your soul in their bodies. This is yet another way to escape pain.

While it is not necessary to know romantic love, your culture has raised this one form to unachievable levels, as it is something perceived as lofty and unattainable— part of some story created by the weak. Again, you have it all backwards.

When you know Love, inside you and in every one you meet in your dimension, when you look past your body-vehicle into the inner light of the soul, you will radiate like a lantern, and others of similar frequency will magnetize to your side like the particles of an atom.

Many of you will first form a partnership of this Love, which will soon create a circle of like-vibrational particles. You have yourself a molecule, as you call it. This is your community, and it is not unlike the makeup of your body, you see.

Your very DNA is charged by Love, and mimics the entirety of each Galaxy, which mimics each part of the Universe. It is like looking at a candle in the mirror, which goes on and on into places and realms and dimensions you may no longer see, but which exist nonetheless. Therefore, you see, you are a part of an ever-expanding Universe of things you cannot yet "see," only because they are beyond you.

When water boils and turns into steam and disappears from your vision, you do not believe it no longer exists, do you? When you turn on a ceiling fan, and it spins fast enough to where you no longer see the blades, you do not believe those same blades disappear, do you? There is no dis-appear. There is only appearance which you are not a vibratory match for.

We, therefore, are not invisible as much as we are not seen by those who have not learned to traject past the life and death cycle into a frequency beyond measure. As you focus on what you don't see more than what you do see, you will bubble up and reach higher heights. Bubble and float, bubble and float, bubble and float—do you understand how easy you can make this?

Focus on your so-called problems and you will sink down, like the yolk of an egg. We have an experiment for you: scramble an egg yolk and observe. (You may cook and eat it if that is your desire to feed your body-vehicle.) Then scramble the whites and watch how they froth and bubble and expand into something else.

Be the egg white. Lift your sights off of the "story" you created, and you will know peace. As you know peace you will inspire others, who are one with the very same spirit as you. You will no longer need violence and suffering—emotional, mental, OR physical—to justify your existence. And when the time comes for you to leave this body behind again, after you heal and reunite with others from your many lifetimes in the circuit, you will now have the inkling that there is something more after the life and death cycle is complete. You have the choice to graduate into dimensions that know of no such thing as suffering.

So choose to leave the suffering behind! Know that it is a choice, despite what you have been told. Haven't you learned enough lessons already? Thinking and believing you must tirelessly repeat the same lessons is child's play.

Rise and know peace.

Q&A - THERE IS NO "TO TRY," THERE IS ONLY "TO BE"

10: Good evening. We are so happy to have you here. What is it you wish to ask?

Q: Why are you called The Power of 10?

A: We together are a super collective of 10 powerful souls, in what you call souls. We choose to not incarnate any longer, and the power of our united front is unique in its creation. The power of who we are is magnified throughout time, and the Universe expands through us and the other souls. That is who we are, and there will be more about this in the coming months.

Q: Why is the Universe so incredibly vast?

A: The Universe is expansive because we make it so. Every thought, every feeling and emotion, creates and expands the boundaries of what you call the *Universe*. The Universe is space, and space is inside of each of us. Space is inside of each of our heads, inside of each thought, inside of each emotion, and every time you create something new, you are expanding the boundaries of the Universe. That is why it is so big, and beyond your comprehension of what is needed.

Q: What relationship are you, or have you, with Abraham?

A: Abraham is a collective conscious, but a separate one from us. We are 10 unique souls brought together as a united front. Abraham is unique in its own consciousness. We are from the same place only different, and we have unique thoughts to share. Abraham has brought consciousness to where it needs to be at the present moment, and we, as The Power of 10, are here to expand on that present moment consciousness, and take it to new levels of existence.

Q: Is the earth and the human race just a primitive form, or almost as an experiment?

A: We, as earth forms, are in a unique position of experimenting with the early laws of attraction. When you expand beyond the boundaries of this present lifetime, you move beyond into places where you may manifest at will. And when you manifest at will, you move beyond into spaces where you may choose to either come back, or choose to go beyond as we have chosen.

When you choose to move beyond, you no longer need a body, and it is in that space and that framework that we provide our own consciousness as expansiveness and magnitude, to new levels—to whole new levels—to where you cannot even conceive.

You are early, but at the same time, you exist on all dimensions of time, and everything is happening in the now at the exact same time, and this is beyond your current level of understanding. So you may listen to these points of attraction, and understand and conceive of what you will, and someday know that you will move beyond into making real what is happening already in the now.

Q: So the understanding of the early phases of attraction is one of the main points that the Universe is trying to clarify?

A: There is no "to try." Understand that there is no "to try." There is simply "to be." In order to expand, you simply stay in the moment, being free of all thought, and feel beyond yourself, your limited "I" self, to beyond into the expansiveness, into the Universe, and each individual soul contributes to the expansive whole of the entire boundaries of the Universe, because in Truth there are no boundaries. It is you who makes it so. There is "no try," there is only "to be."

And expand, and to multiply that "to be." Multiply, as in The Power of 10. Multiply and expand whatever it is you are feeling to the next level of existence. And when you reach the happiest level of freedom, when you know the Truth of what it is to be alive, then you move on to the expansive level of the highest way of being, and you vibrate at a level that is no longer of this earth.

Q: Are there other beings in physical form, as we understand it, in the Universe?

A: We would like to explain the consciousness of, as an example, steam. In your world you have water, and when it vibrates to a higher level, it creates steam, which works into the atmosphere until it gets so heavy, that it drops upon you as rain, and recycles again and again. So steam moves into the atmosphere. So shall you vibrate at higher levels, when you are ready to expand your consciousness and find clarity in the Universe about your wee part, and your creative contribution. And we'd like to focus on that phrase of *creative contribution*. Sit with that particular part of your individual creative contribution to the whole, so eventually you vibrate at a level that you no longer require a body. And you may move into other levels of existence and newer, higher dimensions that do not require the density of your human body.

And, for now, you do choose this level of existence. You choose this body and this adventure, this learning opportunity, that you may move eventually beyond it, and then you will know. You will know the Truth of your existence, and for now, all that is required is that you expand beyond, maybe perhaps one level beyond your current level of existence and knowing, and that is all that is required of you.

Q: I only wrote down one more question, in my attempt to make this a universal question, and that is: How is the best way for people to forgive others who do bad things to each other?

A: It is not necessary to forgive others. The only person that you may forgive is your own self, and your own soul, your own small egoic self. And in the larger sense, anybody that does anything to you is not really true. It is a function of your expansion, and that is all. Once you expand beyond the limited confines of your small being, you will understand why you came forth into this level of your human expansion, so that you may graduate into larger and grander expansions of your real, true being. To move beyond, and to multiply and *expand* to whole new levels of happiness and freedom, and it is a word beyond happiness that you humans have no comprehension of.

There is only a letting go. There is only a detachment of what you feel you need as human beings. There is only a presence of being here, now, not portending into the future, or making sense of what has already occurred. There is no need to forgive. You created this human experience to learn and to grow beyond your limited, little self, and therefore, there is no need. Simply be with what is.

What is your question in this moment? Not planned, not focused. Simply be with what comes. You are doing great work in this world. You are expanding by listening to this exchange, and we are so grateful and appreciative for having a voice.

Q: We are very grateful and appreciative to listen to you. And our—my—most powerful question during this process may be: "How do we spread this knowledge when the time is right?" because it is so fulfilling to hear your insights.

A: You are growing accustomed to this vibration. And with each session that we enjoy together, you are growing in expansion and awareness. And when you reach 10 of these sessions, as in The Power of 10, you will know when to expand beyond and share this with the great masses, many of whom will be drawn to you. You will post these on what you call the internet—the connection between you and all the others. You will post this in anonymity, and they will come to you en masse. They will come to you as they grow ready and seek a higher expansion of their own limited vibration.

And as the masses expand, there will still be others who will drop down into lower and lower levels. And it is not expansion and not your concern. They will separate like an egg, and you shall only be focused on the expansion, and you will post, and they will come to you and in great masses. They will respond to our message, which is only growth and expansion and magnitude and great radiant abundance, on ALL levels, not just your wealth. It will move beyond into great levels of ecstatic joy and vibration at levels you currently do not understand, like levels of water to steam and moving beyond. It is our intention to move you into the next level of being, not just here in 2015, but into the beyond, into the next century—moving multiplied into the powers of 10, scientifically moving you, physically moving you, intentionally, spiritually, e-motionally moving you through your e-mo-tion. You're moving through e-mo-tion, feeling. It is all about feeling your way to the next level, and we will guide you there as beings beyond the physical.

Q: Thank you. When shall we talk to you again?

A: We would like to converse with you as often as humanly possible, when you may choose to make time for us, because we come from a place beyond time and space, and we understand that within your limited framework, that there are certain blocks of time that may work best for you. And we have great abundance to share with you, when you are ready to receive us, and Michelle, as she adjusts to our wavelength and is able to receive us in more magnitude. We welcome the possibilities. And we embrace the ability to converse through her, and we encourage you to continue to record these exchanges as we ready you, and ready our message to be relayed to the rest of humanity. We are approaching the time of great Light and unconditional Love. We are rapidly approaching this time, and so whenever you tell us to, and you allow the vibration to come through Michelle's vehicle, we welcome the opportunity with relaxed ease and the grace of understanding. Thank you.

CHAPTER 2

Life and Love

Life and Love are both beautiful things in your experience, and so, we would like to address both this morning and show you ways of appreciating what you have, what you are creating, and what it means to know the Truth.

When you were in between lives, contemplating with your former family members and angels and spirit guides that which your soul most wanted to accomplish, you sought out this particular life story because it appealed to your sense of adventure and creation. You chose the drama, in an attempt to further your soul's evolution, that you might know peace. Your understanding transcends these experiences; however, for now, it is important to simmer in the juices of your own stew.

It is a rainy winter day where Michelle resides. Her brain activity is already contemplating a hot stew for dinner, and last night, she had chili. Such are the random thoughts of sustenance that travel through your brains on any given day. This thought of food is not a bad thing—not at all. As Michelle dreams, she tastes the stew in her mouth, knowing she will make it a reality in the evening by going to the store and purchasing the items needed. She will be in an enjoyable state of presence as she creates the concoction from a recipe, maybe even humming unconsciously. After it all stews and is complete, she and her husband, Jodah, will enjoy a good meal, with all its tastes. And then they will both be full and satisfied.

Such is the case for a life. You start with being present and accepting and appreciating your surroundings. You begin to get a "taste" for what it is you want. You don't worry about it, or place doubts before it, for such things would only get in the way. Michelle didn't worry about NOT getting her stew. She just knew she would gather the ingredients and enjoy the process. In the end, she *knew* she would appreciate the results and gather great joy and satisfaction from the end result. And so, once you have the "taste" for your desire, it is your deep and utter *knowing* that you can have whatever it is you want that will bring it to you, as long as you can enjoy the journey there.

Where we are, this happens at the moment of tasting. In fact, it happens before our collective mouths even water, for we have no mouths any longer, but we remember way back when we did. We simply enjoy instantaneously whatever feeling and emotion we wish to have, which is why the space beyond the afterlife is so completely wondrous.

Imagine, just for a moment that you could have or be or do anything you want RIGHT NOW. You, in human form, probably could not handle it. From where you stand, you might just explode into orgasmic dust.

When you leave the bodily form and transition into the way station, which many call heaven, you can also make, do, or have anything your soul desires. It just takes a little longer, because your focus is still on what you *had* on earth, not on what you truly *are* in that moment.

Once you place your focus on a higher space than what you had on earth, you will see how easy it is to amplify the joyous emotions you experience as you manifest at will, and then you will eventually tire of the game and be able to handle the space where we reside: a place of utter bliss and complete understanding.

Even just KNOWING this fact will amplify your current vibratory state and allow you to manifest things and experiences more peacefully while still in this dimension. Affirm daily that you wish to learn through faith and not suffering. Say it now:

I NOW LEARN THROUGH FAITH AND NOT SUFFERING.

How does it feel to learn through faith?

Many of you have an understanding of the Laws of Attraction. And that is good—very good, in fact. And we would like to add that your thoughts becoming things, your magnetic resonance through time and space reality, is more Truth than Law, for your "laws" connote a negative association for the most part, and involve rules and regulations.

It is a good start to name it a law, however. And now that you have been playing with these laws and watching how your awareness grows because of them, it is time to merge your playing with your knowing to utilize your faith—not just in creating the opposite of suffering, but in knowing you are a magnetic being, and tapping into your soul's highest functioning within the imaginary confines of your existence.

Because, in Truth, there are no limitations other than the ones you impose upon yourself. You tell yourself a story about how those limitations have always been there, and you focus and dwell on why you can't achieve something, and so that becomes your reality. If you chose higher, you'd *be* higher. That is the Truth.

There are no rules here. No one way to do it or to get it wrong. However, you know you're getting it "right" when you are feeling amazing in each moment and things just keep showing up for you. That's the way it's supposed to be while you're here on earth. THAT is the plan—the planet—you signed up for, right?

You recognize that feeling of excitement, when your body-vehicle is literally trembling with joy and anticipation? That's exactly the space you want to be in! Michelle is doing it now, dreaming about her new office space that she is about to move into. We just had to interrupt her preparations to acknowledge this feeling of the body vibrating at a more rapid pace, rising up through joy and bliss, all through the power of the mind.

It is the same when you are in the infatuation stages of your romantic love. You get up in the morning, excited for the day, excited to be ALIVE. You don't care a thing about your so-called "problems" because you are IN LOVE! Your heart beats faster, you're not hungry, the colors of nature appear more vibrant because you see things for how they truly are in Spirit. That is the state you long for—only not for your brother or sister, but for the one soul you recognize within yourself.

You are made of this Love. And when you achieve unconditional union with yourself, even if your lover leaves you, it just won't matter at all because you are in love with Love. Now that you've felt the inklings of how this changes your perception of the world, you can now visualize it with ease, and conjure up the emotions at any time. Do it now. Remember a time when you felt extreme amounts of Love toward a boyfriend or girlfriend, a spouse, a partner, a child, a pet. Conjure it up, summon it up and use all of your senses to make it real. Now imagine the word "AMPLIFY," and witness the new, higher, more rapid vibrations of your body ... what if you stewed in this?

Bathe in these loving, excited vibrations today, and perhaps write down what happens. For when you find yourself slipping, these writings will serve to remind you of how truly powerful you really are.

Q&A - ANIMALS ARE THE HIGHEST VIBRATION

10: Good afternoon. We are so pleased you took the time to talk to us. Do you have a question?

Q: My first question is: why have you chosen us to speak through?

A: The question is a good one. We come through those who have clarity and purpose. We come to a vibrational match to those who can understand, translate, and emit a response. The two of you are a match for our desires. Michelle has the clarity of mind to receive our words. Jodah is the igniter of the responses. Your relationship is one that is smooth and desirous, and therefore we come through to the two of you. You both are equally a part in this mission.

Q: So there are others on the planet that you are coming through?

A: We come through those who receive us. You are the first to let us come through. We emit a message, and it is our desire for it to be translated. You are the only ones enabled to translate at this moment. Anyone who clears their mind in meditation and spends the time to receive *could* receive us, and it is our hope in time that The Power of 10 can make its way to anybody wishing to receive a higher vibrational response to life.

J: We have a loud cat.

10: Animals are the highest vibrational creatures there are. So many of you believe that they are lower in energy, and they are not. They are clear-minded and they Love unconditionally, and you would do well to emulate your "pets" as you call them.

J: That's good to hear. We've had discussions like that before.

Q: Can you please expand on your example from last night about how water turns to steam, and as the steam becomes so dense it then falls back down on this planet? Is the rain that falls—is the existence of the earth—the rain in that example?

A: In our example, vibrationally your humans rise up like water to steam, and as the vibration recycles it moves back into the density that is your body. Earth itself, she has a cycle, and her energy is created from all those who inhabit her. We would like to discuss resistance to the cycle. It is only through your resistance, through your blocking of the raising of your frequency that brings you down. If you were to choose to continue to rise upwards, there would be no density, and therefore no need to inhabit the earth. You would continue to rise and to vibrate until you were invisible, as we are. We cannot be seen by the naked eye. We can only be felt and translated. We are non-physical in form. You are still physical and require the density of a planet to plant your feet, to feed you, to nourish you. Therefore, water to steam to sky and beyond into space is the trajectory we would encourage— not to drop again into density as you so far are doing. Do you understand?

J: Yes, thank you.

10: Of course.

Q: Also, last night you made it a point to separate the syllables of the word "e-mo-tion." We've also had some discussion of this in past months. Can you elaborate on that as well?

A: Yes. The emotions you feel are energy into motion. They are your feelings, and your guide to what is currently occurring in your own vibration. It is key; it is your knowledge. It is a point of existence that you can move. E-motion is energy in motion. So many of you are in resistance to your emotion, and therefore, you block your movement into the next realm of your existence into higher vibrational frequencies that may be multiplied into pure happiness, and joy, and bliss. Why you would do that would be fear—fear and anger, the lower emotions. The higher emotions of bliss, and joy, and appreciation magnify. That is something we would like to focus on in the coming sessions, for it is that trajectory that will take you higher to a place that will change humanity—where no longer will you have such violence—and you will move your emotions to the higher vibration that will bring peace within you, and peace throughout all of your peoples to a place where you will no longer harm each other.

J: Thank you.

10: You are most welcome.

Q: We also spoke of the nature of contrast vs. example in people's lives. Can you give us your thoughts on that?

A: Yes. In the past, you have all learned through contrast. You learn and grow from what you don't want as much as what you do want. Yes? And, there are those who teach by example. There have been the great masters throughout time—your Jesus, or Buddha, or Krishna, or Gandhi—there are many, many more—Mohammed, who have been high vibrational, who have chosen perhaps to no longer incarnate to learn their lessons. They understood how to teach by living, and those were the best ways back in history. As you progress, you will someday no longer need contrast. It is *not* always a given. It is the way you must learn as of now. Eventually, you will no longer need this. You will no longer need it. You will *live* it, because you will know that there is nothing else except for unconditional Love. It is the Truth of who you are, and anything else will feel foreign to you. It is our gift to you, our gift to present to you that, yes, right now you require contrast to learn from its opposite, and it is our absolute promise to you that in time, you will get to a frequency where that is no longer a part of your vibration. And then, and only then, will you have complete peace and harmony that comes from the place where no contrast is needed.

Q: Is the message that you want to spread through us something that the humans can get to that place of no contrast? Or is that only after we are not dense enough to have bodies?

A: Our message to you is one of peace. Peace has no opposite. Peace is a place of space and happiness and bliss that vibrates at such a high space that your recycling is no longer needed. When you choose to no longer fall into the abyss that is the lower moving vibrations, then yes, you will reach *our* place: a place where it is only a choice to come back.

You may still choose the adventure of feeling contrast to learn, but it is indeed a choice. It is not a given, as you've been told. It may take, in what you see in time, as centuries. We come to you now to plant the seeds of peace, because it is important that you know it is possible.

J: That warms my heart to hear that it is possible.

10: Good. It is indeed possible.

Just hearing these words we feel your vibration lifting, and it is our hope that by transmitting these messages of Truth, of knowing, of setting an example of who *we* are and who we have attained, that your human folks will reach the same place. At some point, you all will. Or you will choose to come back. And in that case, there will become two worlds. A world as we said before—a separation as in an egg yolk to the white. Neither is good or bad; it's just very different. As you choose to move higher up in your emotions, to the point where your energy is vibrating so very high that you are not even seen, you will disappear from the level of lower violence that is becoming Earth. It is a place, a kindergarten of learning. And there will be some souls who choose the drama, who choose to stay in contrast, and that is okay. And it is important that you do not judge them. For if you judge, you will sink down to that level, and sinking is again part of the recycling. Recycling isn't very fun now, is it?

J: (Laughs) No it is not.

Q: Are there steps that we should be taking while we are in these first sessions?

A: The only thing you must focus on is being fully present to the lessons. We appreciate your recording of them, and it is very important that you keep these very private, until the count of 10 sessions has occurred. And then you will release them, and once again, the people will come to you. There is no need to force anything to happen. Nothing happens by force. I will say that again: Nothing happens by force. I am one of the 10. I am the "leader," if you will. My name is Myagana, and I will be speaking more to you. We will be taking turns and each one of us holds a separate vibration. Together, they form a cohesive whole.

Do you have more questions?

J: I don't think I do right now. I'm just enjoying this interaction.

10: As are we. You have some concerns about Michelle's health, yes?

J: (Laughs) Yes.

10: She is going to be okay. We are raising her vibration to meet ours, so that she may be in a position to reach us. She only has to do nothing. She sometimes fights having her body be used for this purpose, and we understand and appreciate her receptivity. She will, in time, grow accustomed, and we will work on her as she sleeps. Your Love for her will help her in this process. It is one of the main reasons we chose the two of you, for your Love is that of the highest nature.

J: That's the one thing I'm sure of here.

Q: Will I have more time in order to devote to spreading this message soon, without having to spend time making what we call "money?"

A: Time is only an illusion. We understand your human difficulty in attaining balance. This mission will not take up much of your time, and it is an important one for people to understand. Without it, you will continue to drop down as the yolk into the earth. With it, you will continue to rise into the higher vibrational ethers, where there is no need to do what you call "work," which is usually of a lower vibration. You will gravitate toward the things that give you peace and happiness and joy. If your job, as you know it, brings you those feelings, you are rising up. And if it does not, then you are lowering down. You must find a way to be neutral, to find and carve the space and time to record our sessions, and put them out. That does not take a lot of your time, no?

J: No.

10: At some point, we would like to put this down in writing, and it shall be direct. There is no need for you to edit—it will be exact in our directions. When that time comes, you will have plenty of time in your other endeavors, for through the law of attraction, you will create the exact conditions conducive to achieving all of our aims.

J: That sounds perfect.

10: Good.

You have many, many blessings rained down on you. You don't know how to receive them. That will be our learning as well, our teaching to you. Receive. Being receptive is a gift. Making things happen never, never works. There is another in our Power of 10; her name is Eudicine. And she will address the push/pull dance of making things happen versus allowing things to be received. It is a very important tenet of The Power of 10 to multiply your blessings. When you learn how to receive and allow, you will be again floating in the higher vibrations. There will no longer be a need to do what you call "work." Even the word is of a lower vibration.

J: Thank you.

10: You are very welcome. Thank you for your so-called "time." We look forward to our next encounter.

CHAPTER 3

God as Love

Now this is going to make you really mad.

Anger is also of a strong vibratory nature, and so it is okay if you are mad for a little while with us. All we ask is that you stay in a state of neutrality until you hear us out. See if what we say next resonates within your soul. Perhaps channel your anger into passion, which feels much, much better. At any rate, what we say next will not lead you into depression, which is just about the lowest place you can go.

What if God was also a collective group of highly evolved souls, such as us? What if you did not personify your God, because at your heart of hearts you understand this force is not male or female, despite your picture books? We will not call God a "he" or "she" because God is Love and of a much higher vibration than needs housing in a body.

You are God, and God is you. God is even higher than we are, yet it is all happening at once, and not in a linear mountain as you may conceive of us. We are also God, and God dwells within and around us, for we no longer have a body.

If you take the personification out of the God, you may understand more easily why God would never have belief systems such as you [do]. God understands itself as unconditional Love, and so moving forward, we will only refer to the name of God AS Love.

You have placed too many negative connotations on something that is so beautiful and beyond your level of understanding. This Creative Divine Source of all creation would never hate, never fear. Love does not hate. Love does not fear. Get it?

Love also doesn't just give you everything you want in the way you want it in the moment. That could be disastrous, given where you are from our standpoint.

We would like to give you an example. Michelle and Jodah are on a detoxifying cleanse, which is good for the body and soul. Interestingly enough, in the beginning, they were both instructed to eat as much fat as their stomachs could handle. The idea is to flush the body of toxins and encourage the body to burn more fat. They had both done it in the past, and it worked well, with good results.

So they were both eager to eat ravenously everything "off limits" for a short while, until it became gross to them, and they felt dense and awful. That's what happens when you feed the body vehicle heavy foods. Your vibration temporarily lowers, your mind gets foggy, even your soul becomes clouded. You want to sleep and lack motivation.

Once they began eating lighter fruits and vegetables and proteins, their bodies felt much cleaner and lighter. Their minds became sharp again, and they connected more freely with ideas and others who vibrate at a higher level.

Your mind and individualized ego may think it wants those foods because of the taste, but it is a temporary pleasure, an addictive high. A much better approach is to look at things from our broader perspective, from the "bigger picture," as you call it. Meter out your sense pleasures, and you will have a calmer, happier existence while you are learning and growing in this dimension. We encourage you to take baby steps, as it will feel better from where you are at.

Once you reach the way station you call heaven, things will appear to speed up due to your lack of a dense body. And they will speed up and vibrate even faster once you direct your soul in our direction. You will attain everything and every experience your heart desires, as long as you take this process lightly. Don't force it to happen all at once, or your body-vehicle might overheat.

Another example we would like to give is of a toddler or a small child who wants for toys. You may feel like you want to give them everything because of your Love for them. And yet, small children do not yearn for anything other than sustenance, and protection, and the return of their unconditional Love toward you! If you gave them everything they wanted all at once, they would likely throw a tantrum. They are happier with the boxes the toys come in. Isn't that the Truth?

And so, if you were given all the earthly "toys" here on earth, you might act like a spoiled child, and no one would want to remain in your midst. That is far worse than gathering "things." Enjoy the journey as you bring into the material world your wants and desires one at a time. Learn to savor them, as you would a good dish, slowly and using all the senses. Please don't make this dimensional reality all about hoarding your stuff. You chose this life for the inherent magic in manifesting thought into form. How fun! Be playful and celebrate as each thing and experience and opportunity and person enters your life story. Be happy you wrote them into the script.

And, for some reason, if you feel at the end of your life story that you did not do or accomplish all that you believe you wanted out of it, either write a new story or instantaneously create it at the way station until you get it out of your system. You can also choose to reincarnate into this particular life form—to repeat kindergarten so to speak. It will not hold you back. Not in the least. There is no such thing as time, remember? You have all the time of eternity. When you tire of creating your things and experiences, you will eventually opt for the space where we reside—or even beyond us. You may choose to observe and guide and teach, as we have chosen. Or you may go beyond and blend into Love.

It is always your choice.

Focus

Your mind is a tool, and yet, it is all over the place.

It is important to learn how to rein in your thoughts before you reach the space where we reside, because if you constantly change your mind, you will not receive the experience you were longing for as you chose to incarnate into this dimension.

Again, we use the example of kindergarteners, not because we wish to be patronizing, but because they are so cute in their endeavors, and mimic how cute we think you are as you go through this expansion into the great beyond.

Your kindergartners have an abundance of energy, and they are all over the map, always running, and painting, and laughing, and crying, and changing toys and friends, and such. They have not yet learned how to sit still, and so they are given the freedom to create and explore, while at the same time given some rudimentary structure so that they may concentrate on building knowledge.

You, too, should be given such freedom, and you have been—you just don't always recognize it as such. If you viewed your "work" as you do a kindergartener's "play," you might just take it all so much more lightly. If a kindergartener gets bored of his or her activity, they just abandon it for something new. In the same manner, if a job isn't helping you learn, grow, or have fun, you can leave it at any time and start something else that makes you feel excited.

However, just as scattered as a young child can get, when they do find something that enthuses their spirit, they can play with it for hours, or even days and weeks and months. When they find a movie they enjoy, they can watch endlessly, and laugh at the same places, and learn new things at each viewing.

In the same way, once you find something that excites you, if you harness your attention toward that thing, or experience, or person, you will have great satisfaction, and a sense of fulfillment and peace. That is what we want you to be after! Passion, then peace.

In our environment, these things and souls and experiences happen very rapidly, quicker than your current level of understanding. Everything flows, and our thoughts instantaneously form a reaction. If that thought would be negative, you would not even be able to reach where you are. You might heal first in the way station of heaven, or even come back into various life stories before you stop thinking in critical terms which separate.

So you can see, it is of extreme importance that you learn focus. How does one do this, you ask?

Here is a tool for you, if you wish to reach the pinnacle of your lifetime here and into the great beyond of faster dimensions that produce pure bliss.

It is all about the eyes.

You were given EYES! Isn't that amazing? If you put more focus on your eyes, as the seer of the soul, than your body vehicle, things would change dramatically for you. Rather than just casually looking at things, why not really gaze at a flower, or a sunset, or a tree? Gaze into your lover's eyes without laughing or looking away. Really do it! If you don't have a lover, look into a child's eyes, and see the spark of awareness that you share. Gaze and behold, gaze and behold.

Then, when you find yourself in a state of awe of this very simple experiment, AMPLIFY this feeling times 10, and see where that takes you. Anytime you find your emotions have risen to a place of contentment or beyond, focus on the amplification of that feeling and you will have an inkling of who and what we are in every moment. Do that enough, and your inklings will turn into a highly evolved lifetime, which should translate very easily into a higher dimension when the time comes.

You may choose to stop reading here for the time being, and bask in your state of bliss. Pause and renew, and then try the following experiment on a new day.

As you open your eyes first thing in the morning, remind yourself that it is your soul looking out of the body vehicle. Focus your awareness on your soul as the one who is seeing throughout the day. Gaze a little longer at each thing you see, as if it is the first or last time you are witnessing such beauty. Others may look askew at you, perhaps thinking you quite odd in the moment. So perhaps begin with sharing your experience with other people who might understand this experience and grow from the encounter as well.

Document your observations, and return to them when you forget who you are. You are at the start of a journey that spans multiple dimensions—the spark of a flame that never burns out.

Q&A - We guarantee it is better than your orgasms

10: Good evening. We are so very thrilled that you came back. You have questions for us? We have answers.

J: We have questions ranging from deeper questions to just curiosities.

10: Start with the easiest ones.

Q: If you were [incarnate], when did you experience a lifetime on earth?

A: We have experienced many, many lifetimes on your planet. Together all of us have come back over and over through your recycling plan. That is how we know we no longer need to return. We learn; we move on. And we have all been in your shoes—every single one of us.

Q: We enjoy what we call "earthly pleasures," such as food, and laughter, and sex. Is there an equivalent of that where you are, or is it something even beyond?

A: When you move beyond your so-called death, there is a place where you experience some of the same pleasures as you call them. You reach a realm wherever whatever you think instantaneously appears. You have that very same power now; you just don't realize it all the time. When you move beyond dimensions to the higher state which we would like you to attain, it is such a high state you do not any longer seek temporary pleasures. We are beyond temporary pleasures. It is of a joy and a bliss you cannot currently conceive of, and we guarantee it is better than your orgasms!

Q: Why are you contacting us? Why are you wanting humanity to move forward under your guidance?

A: It is time. It is the time of separation: the time where there are many of you ready to move beyond, en masse. In prior history, that was not the case. We, The Power of 10, are teachers. We have lived your lives. We have gone through your suffering and your pains. It is difficult, if not impossible, to watch you suffer. There is no longer a need. You were very, shall we say "primitive," in your response to life, and you have grown up enough to realize higher states of being. It is time! It is time, and because it is time, you are now able to receive us. It is only a matter of you being ready to receive, not us being ready to give.

Q: This idea of oneness that brings peace in the individual and the collective consciousness, how will this mindset of oneness be spread throughout a world that is so based in ego right now?

A: Oneness is a state of Truth, not conception. It is time to peel back all the many layers of ego, until we reach our core, which is the Truth of who we are. The Truth is Oneness. We are all shared consciousness. We, once more, do not have to force anything. All is being remembered. As you grow, as you multiply—as in, again, The Power of 10 as a concept—you will grow and multiply and vibrate so much higher that the others will see and grow, or fall behind and perish. It is not for you to judge. It is simply for you to separate.

We understand that the idea of separateness and oneness seems at opposite ends. However, those of you who remember your oneness, remember your Truth, will come together. And those who remain in separateness will simply have to go at it much longer. In the meantime, their suffering will beget more suffering. The key is not to sink with them. You cannot help someone by sinking into their mud. You must rise, rise, rise. Use the word, your word rise. Say it until you feel it. It is one of the techniques that we shall give to you, is to use your language, to use your words, as each word carries a particular vibration. Perhaps for you it is rise. No one can argue with the word rise.

J: One of my questions was going to be what are examples of ways we can raise our vibration?

10: There you go.

J: Thank you.

10: That is one. We will share more in coming months, when you are ready. Begin with rise. Keep it simple.

J: Ok.

Q: Yesterday you talked about how the only thing is not to force, but to receive. Can you tell me more about how to receive?

A: Yes, it is more about being in the receptive mode. You know the moment before you wish to create something. If you are feeling empowered by the creation, you will be inspired to move forward. If you are not, if you are feeling any other emotion besides inspiration or creation, then it is something that must rest. You must take a moment to rest, to meditate, to clear your mind, to be in flow, and then receive instructions on how to next be guided.

Your world is so concerned with making something happen in every single moment. If you would just take a step back, take five minutes of your time—five—you will know what to do. Inspired = high vibration. Forcing = no good vibration. You know the difference. Even your lower vibe people know the difference. Take five minutes before you act.

J: I was going to ask you about when is the time to take action, but as you speak I realize that how we typically define action is forcing something. And so, what you are saying is to meditate or to take those five minutes, and then that inspiration is then the right time to take action?

10: Yes. Being in a receptive mode is everything. We wish we could take the word "force" out of your vocabulary. There is no need. Imagine a world without force. How would that world feel? It is not up to you or anybody to force anybody to do anything. It is not up to your God, to Universe, to Source Energy, whatever you call your Creator, to force you to do anything. You are so much more powerful than you even realize. However, that power may be misguided. Allowing is the magic. Allowing is what will bring peace to your world.

Q: You mention the word "God." So many people here, and I'm sure you know this from your time, have such a different idea about who or what God is. Can you tell us what your experience, your insight, into this concept, is?

A: Perhaps the word "God" is simply too loaded. It is unfortunate. You may interchange the word God with the word Love. Every single person can accept the word Love. If we all prayed to Love, instead of praying to various aspects of God, we would be— you would be—a better world. We are beyond the world. (Laughs) We do not mean to make fun of you. It is just so absurd that you all break into fights over who created you. It doesn't matter. You are all made of Love, you will all return to Love, and Love will shoot you into the trajectory beyond life and death.

J: You're right, it is absurd.

10: When you are feeling low emotion, when you are feeling sad, or mad, or frustrated, if you would remember to come back to a place of Love, if you would remember how you feel around your animals, how you felt as a young child, how you feel in nature, how you feel with a romantic partner who cares deeply about you—all of these things bring you closer to the definition of who you really are. It would be good for you to remember this more often and remind each other. Perhaps use the word "Love" instead of the word "God," and see how the world changes.

Q: There are—completely shifting gears—there are a lot of people who talk about travelling through time. And we think as humans in such a linear fashion, but we were talking about last night that perhaps time travel is not based in a human life, but rather, since all time is simultaneously happening, do we essentially, in recycling—is that time travelling?

A: Yes and no. You humans think in linear terms, and you also think in physical terms. When you imagine time travel in your television shows, and movies, and books, you see machines, you see bodies. Again, we are beyond form. We are non-physical entities beyond life and death. Once you do not have a body, you do not need to move anywhere. You instantaneously are everywhere and nowhere all at the same time. If you choose—and it is a choice—to return to earth, to move through the adventure you call life, you can go backwards, you can go forward, you can go into different places at the same time. The soul has no bounds. The soul can be in more than one body at the same time. We understand your difficulty understanding this, but it is the Truth. Your soul is unlimited. It is a part of Spirit; it is a part of Love, or God, or Universe, or Source Creation. It is a part of all that is. You don't need a machine. You don't need to use a body. Once you move beyond the body, you can go anywhere you want, anytime you want. It is really fun.

J: (Laughs) I'm sure. I look forward to it.

Q: I have to ask this. Is there something with peanut butter recently, and us talking to you?

A: Peanut butter is a craving that Michelle has for protein. Her body is expending great amounts of energy, as you have talked about. She will adjust. It is all a part of the energy moving. Allow her to have her cravings. She is in tune with her body and knowing what it wants. She will adjust. We would like to take this time to reaffirm that she will not only be okay, she will thrive. Her higher vibrational energy will create radiant health. All of you, as you raise your vibrational energy, will first create radiant health, which is one of the first things that many of you seek, and should be the first thing you seek. Without radiant health, what else can you possibly have?

When you traject beyond a body, you don't have to worry about health; you can focus on other things. And while you are in a body, your cells must reach a point of vibration, where there is no more sickness. We would like to give you that hope as well, that as you vibrate at the higher pace, that is the key to all well-being. That is the key to all health—it's a higher vibration. And in each moment, you may lift it up, beginning with the use of the word rise.

Q: Yesterday you talked about when there is no resistance, there is no effort needed to raise the vibration. So, what you are saying is the natural state, without us getting in the way, basically is that higher trajectory?

A: It is like a beach ball in the water. It takes much more energy to hold the beach ball in the water. If you let it go, it will fly in the air. The same is with your energy. When you block it, you are expending a lot of unnecessary energy. If you just let go, you would shoot into the air like a cork in a champagne bottle. And, in addition, you may use tools until you learn how to get out of your own way. Tools are not a bad thing. Using the word rise is one of those. You must catch yourself in the process of blocking. Once it is there, and you notice it, you observe it—you notice you are blocking, you say to yourself "rise up, rise up, rise up," and watch how your body feels. Each time this will get easier, until there is a time you don't need to say rise anymore. You will just know.

J: Thank you, that's good.

10: You are welcome.

Q: Has the balance of peace and violence that we see in today's world—has that always been similar, or can we just find out more about what's going on in the world with technology now?

A: There has always been a yin and a yang: a positive and negative polarity of peace and violence on the planet. They have not been worse; they have not been better. They have remained the same for all these years. People have harmed each other in various ways, with different weapons of violence. You are right when you say now you have massive forms of media that show horrible images that stay in your mind and create more violence. Violence begets violence. Negative vibe and fear creates more fear. When people are fearful, they become dangerous. Your goal is simply to rise beyond the violence into higher and higher forms of joy. Peace is a part of joy, so no. It is not different. What's different is you are. What's different is this time. People are tired of the dynamic. There are many who no longer wish to be part of the dramatic, part of the linear, fearful, traumatic times. As more of you awaken to your true powers, to your oneness, to your understanding, to the Love that is you, you will move beyond, and you will attract more and more to The Power of 10. We are using this name because it is a time, of not just moving to the next level, but moving 10 x 10 x 10 x 10. It is time for the Universe to expand beyond your limited understanding. You do not need to convince those of your peace. You need only *be* peace. The others will see it, and they will likely go deeper down. They cannot handle your Light. That is not your decision. Your choice is to move into your Light, to shine even brighter, the Truth of who you are, to a place where nothing can harm you anymore because, guess what? When you no longer have a body, no one can shoot you, no one can cut you. When you don't have a body, nothing can harm you. And when nothing can harm you, you live in a sense of safety and peace beyond your current level of understanding. Without a body, there is no fear.

Q: When our vibration becomes high enough, is that when we die on this planet as we know it, or do we disappear in a cloud of mystical smoke?

A: You make us smile. It is not like in your movies. To others you will appear to die. Your body will appear to pass as you know it. However, you will not truly die. You will leave your body behind. Instead of going to your version of life after death, you will transcend to a higher dimension, to a much broader, expansive version of life. It is there where we reside. When you die currently, it is a sort of "way station." It is school. It is healing and vacation, until you choose to come back. It is like a bus stop.

We move beyond that. We go where we are needed. We teach. Our collective teaches. Others do other things, which we will talk about in coming months. We do not want you to try to grasp too much all in one evening. But to answer your question, it will look as if your body has perished to all others. And once you move beyond, into the ever-transcendent now, you will join others who have left their bodies behind as well, and join you in triumphant peace and joy and happiness.

J: That makes me smile.

10: Smiling is of a high vibration. When you move beyond the physical, your smile is energetic. You have more questions for us?

J: I wrote down more questions, but they don't seem to be as important as the idea of raising vibration and smiling.

10: Eudicine would like to speak for a few moments if that would be all right with you.

J: That would be wonderful, thank you.

10: I am here to speak of ebb and flow. You have brought that up tonight and this evening, and for that, I am very grateful. It is the idea, just like the ocean, that there are tides of movement, and times to recede. This is a very receptive time in your Universe. It is a time of more feminine qualities. I have taken on more feminine qualities. However, all of us, all 10 of us, have been various genders and races throughout time. I project more feminine qualities, to project more receptivity. We would like for you all to experiment, before the next session, with receptivity for just a day, or a week, or a month—whatever unit of time you wish. Play with the notion of allowing things to be exactly as they are: allowing people to be exactly as they are, allowing each moment to be exactly as it is. Do not try to force anything. When you find that you want to make something happen, stop and take five minutes to meditate and clear your mind, and then return to whatever it is you were planning to do. Whenever you feel the urge to do, remember to rest. Your world needs more rest. If you rested more, you would be happier. You're doing too much. That is all I'd like to say at this time. There will be much more at later months. Thank you.

J: Thank you.

10: And we understand you may have difficulty pronouncing my name. You may call me "E."

J: Your name is beautiful.

10: Thank you. I like it.

J: Eudicine.

10: Eudicine.

J: Thank you for talking to us tonight.

10: Thank you for receiving us. We have great Love for you.

CHAPTER 4

Relationships

It would be very good for us to discuss with you the power of your relationships, and why you have them on this dimension.

When you enter into an agreement with another, whether through friendship or marriage or partnership, you observe those qualities in yourself through their behavior and motives. If you do not like what it is you are witnessing, it is simply a sign that you are moving onto a different frequency where they are not at. Alternatively, they could be moving onto a differing vibration, and you would do wise to catch up with them.

Other souls are a barometer for your own vibrational level. It is at this stage in your development that it is so crucial to interrelate with your species, in order to further your understanding of your own soul as one unit, expressing myriad ways.

Do you wish to travel farther than you've ever gone before? Do you wish your life to be the grand adventure you signed up for before your entry into this worldly dimension? Of course you do!

And if you were to undertake any great journey, you would likely have buddies, yes? Fellow travelers who may assist you in getting to your destination. And so it is essential that you magnetically attract those who might further you to your highest vibrational attainment on this planet, and leave behind those who might serve to drag you down.

This is not selfish. We find that to be a stupid word. Of course, when you are mired in ego that is one thing, but that is not the lesson we are trying to communicate with you here. Being in a state of fully expressing your highest Self in each moment is the surest way to satisfaction, and the path that leads to where we are— beyond life and death and suffering.

If others on your path choose a vibration to land at, that is their concern and not yours. By living the highest example of your soul's purpose, you will radiate bliss and peace, and those in your midst will either step it up to meet your rpm, or bounce off.

Your body is the perfect representation of this. Both healthy cells and destructive cells can multiply, based on the greater whole. One "bad" cell can't do much, but if it proliferates, it can cause rampant destruction, even death of the body as you know it.

In the same way, one lower-vibing person can only cause destruction if you move in closer. Choose a healthy, vibrant group of people who are circulating faster, and you will know peace.

What this means is you can't stay in a miserable relationship and be a happy person, right? You must know this, as it is a rudimentary concept to grasp, and yet you do it all the time, believing you can alter their course. That is ego, thinking you must change another's vibration. That path is most certainly up to them. Your interference is not needed or tolerated. Move on and be free.

Whether this is in marriage or friendship or work situations or even clubs and hobbies, it makes no difference. They are showing you where you *were*, not where you are at.

Conversely, if you look into their eyes and only see Love, this is the highest attainment and will assist you in more rapidly attaining a magnetic vibratory state, which may just traject you straight into the frequency beyond! When you are with such people, your energy level increases exponentially, and it is at this time which you should AMPLIFY those feelings times 10! It will make you giddy with joy, which is what you are after ... which is what we are all about.

Moving into joy does not have to be "hard." In fact, it is the easiest thing you can do here where you stand. If you need to be alone while doing this, so be it. A brief time alone will help you gather the momentum you need for positive, like-minded others to seek you out.

Cut the strings that bind you! What is stopping you? Making excuses about hating your job, or your partner, or your living space is a fool's game. Don't participate, as it's all an illusion you created before birth anyway. Deep down, this resonates with you.

And yet, you struggle. You say you have to "pay the bills." From where we stand, there are no mandatory bills. If you must, simplify your life into the basics of planetary and bodily needs: food, shelter, clothing. Beyond that level of comfort is your freedom, and we assure you, once you release the need to control your environment so much, others who "hear" the calling of your frequency will be throwing food, shelter, and clothing at you! And once you have your fill of such things, you may "throw" these things at others, so that humanity will rise together, having their most basic needs met.

And, of course, we have shared before that when you meet the space where we are, you need none of these things. In fact, you don't need them in the way station either, yet many of the souls who shed their bodies will still long for them. When you reach the multiplied state of The Beyond, you won't desire, because you will no longer need a body to clothe, feed, and shelter, and you will no longer require sensory pleasures to make you happy. You will be ready for a continual state of bliss and complete understanding.

But for now, you just aren't ready. And that is okay. We are here to hold your collective hands through the process into eventual spiritual graduation.

Eudicine, one of our 10, says that in order to let go, one must learn the state of flow and surrender, flow and surrender, flow and surrender. Say this 10 times per day, "flow and surrender," and write down what that means for you. She will be speaking more on this in upcoming chapters.

Q&A - IMAGINE SIMPLY UNZIPPING YOUR BODY

10: Good evening.

J: Good evening. Last time you told me to start with the easy questions.

10: That is right.

Q: You said at one point that perhaps you are the leader or the spokesperson. How does that work?

A: We are a collective of 10. Myagana is the one who coordinates, the one who gains the stream of energy that reaches down to Michelle. We all no longer have bodies; we are beyond the physical as we have mentioned before. However, there is always a place of hierarchy. Myagana chose to have us come together, as we are all of a similar frequency. It is easy for us to amplify our powers together. We all represent different aspects of the collective unconscious, and Myagana makes sure that we all vibrate at the same high level and that we choose who to come through based on the evidence of their clarity.

Q: So if Eudicine is speaking of ebb and flow, every other one will speak to us on a different topic?

A: When the Divine timing is right, sometimes Eudicine will speak—when the time is right. We may not get to all 10. It, as you say, depends.

Q: Will we be sharing these initial recordings with the world or will we start sharing after the tenth conversation?

A: You are very impatient. We will tell you when you get to number 10. How does that sound?

J: That sounds fine. You know I'm curious.

10: We are still getting used to the vibration of Michelle and using her body to emit our mission and messages. Your curiosity is welcomed and is part and parcel of the reason we chose both of you. Therefore, do not apologize. You are just getting ahead of yourselves.

Q: What are what we call angels and spirit guides here? Everybody seems to have a different opinion about what they are.

A: That is a very good question. What you call angels are very high vibrational creatures. They are like us in that they are non-physical entities. At the same time, they have never been born and never recycled in each incarnation. Spirit guides are somewhat higher in frequency as they have gone in and out of the incarnations. They sometimes think they will join us, and then they choose to come back. There are certain lessons that they can only learn through suffering. Or they perhaps choose to have certain creature comforts. They are like us in their mission to teach. However, they come back for a specific soul because they know their soul in their entirety. They have been with them. Perhaps they Love them. They want to see them succeed. And it is their sincere hope that at some point the person will recognize them and remember who they are, and ask for their assistance out loud, because it is a violation of free will for them to surpass the person's free will. And so they must ask, and it is their hope that they remember.

We, as the collective, have chosen the trajectory straight out of the recycling and are beyond that. So, while we have the same vibratory level as the angels, we are not the same. We enjoy conversing with them, and it is our great joy to meet with them often.

Q: Thank you. The other day when you said that pets were a way to raise one's vibration and that feeling, that Love that is pure and unconditional ... is that the reason that the animals are here with us on earth?

A: We are all here, or I shall say, you are all here, to raise your vibrational frequency, to rise up—all of you: every single creature on earth. You are here to enjoy the process, to Love unconditionally, as that is the Truth of your being. Animals, humans—no difference. They just are not in their mind like you are.

This is Myagana speaking. I chose to come through because I have a fondness for animals. They, too, choose to go beyond body and become our precious friends. They are with us in Spirit as well. That is what you call your "spirit animals." You are familiar with that form?

J: I am not, but there are probably many who are ...

10: That is how I would define it. They are simply Spirit—animals' souls moving into Spirit—and guiding us and comforting us and not over-thinking.

J: It's ironic that there's so much information to absorb, and one of the most important things is to not think too much about it.

10: It is all about leaning your way into a vibratory state. Your thinking begins the process, like a spark to a flame. However, the feeling leads beyond into the frequency, and the frequency is the most important thing to pay attention to.

You may retrace your steps, if you find your vibratory state is not satisfactory. You may trace it backwards. Ask yourself: "I am feeling dull. What am I feeling? I am feeling not so good. What am I thinking? I am thinking negative thoughts. How can I change this?" Then maybe you pet your cat.

That is why the pets are higher in their vibratory state. They do not go through those levels. They do not think, they do not feel, they go straight to vibration. You should do well to mimic your pets.

J: Thank you, I've not heard that correlation between the thinking and the feeling—that's wonderful. I've enjoyed also telling myself to rise up, and Eudicine's instructions about taking a moment to allow creativity ... my mind's blank, and I can't think of the word. You probably know what I'm trying to say. Before acting on something, to take that moment to center myself ...

10: Are you speaking of inspiration?

J: Thank you.

10: Yes. How is that working for you?

J: It feels peaceful when there's that moment of feeling like I should or need to be doing something, and then waiting for the inspiration. It's just a feeling of peace and surrender knowing that it will be the right time.

10: And that is the seedlings of peace. You are starting to notice. That is good.

Now, taking it one step further, tracing backwards when you have a vibratory state, and you trace it back to the feeling to, as you say—should do something, need to do something, forcing something to happen. Tracing it back to the thought—what is the thought behind that feeling? Will the world fall apart if you do not act on what you think you need to do at the moment? No.

That is ego. As Eudicine points out, take the five minutes. That's all you need. Or you take 10 minutes, or you take 20 minutes. Time is no matter. You take the time until your vibratory state is high. You perhaps listen to music, or take a walk outside, until you reach a place where you feel high. When you do, it will not feel so necessary. It will feel calm and perhaps even energizing; whereas just five minutes before you felt compelled to do something, now it comes from a state of grace. When you have a moment such as this, remember to amplify it times 10. That is The Power of 10. What does it feel like to traject your emotions in this way? Take that feeling of peace now, and the next time it comes over you, multiply it times 10. And take a snapshot of that memory. That is your high vibratory state. And it is what we are encouraging you to reach.

J: I like that.

10: We do also.

Q: One last question for the evening, because I know I'll speak with you tomorrow. When we spoke before of the concept of oneness in the world and people realizing that that's where we needed to be, it's really—isn't it more about not exactly the concept of oneness, but once more people realize the Truth about what and who they are, which is pure Love, that the oneness is almost a byproduct of that?

A: Yes and no. Oneness is Love. Oneness is what your soul enters into. Once you drop the body, oneness is who you are. It is space. It is space times 10. Everything in the Universe is made up of tens. You shall know this when you pass, and you've known it many times as you are old souls, many of you. If you have not figured it out yet, you will when you pass this incarnation.

So something you can do as a tool, is to imagine simply unzipping your body, imagining all the skin dropping to the ground. Your soul steps out of the body. What is it now? It is oneness with all that is. That is who you are. There is no denying this. You may take that soul and multiply it. It is time to traject; you are taking too long. You insist on recycling again and again, and you were never meant to do it that many times. It is like repeating the same grade in your schooling education. At some point, you need to graduate and move into the real world, which is that of Spirit and space beyond time, beyond recycling, beyond incarnations—*beyond*. That is a place where we are, where we exist together.

Sometimes, we focus to get across certain ideas, certain aspects of the collective unconscious. That is why we speak in singular terms. We are more powerful together, as are you. Someday you will know this; hopefully sooner rather than later. That is why we come to you now. You are at the very beginnings of this knowledge, and it's time to multiply it.

Utilize the Law of Attraction, not just to gather material things, which will never give you true, lasting joy. They are only trinkets and temporary pleasures. Beyond this is so much more. So start by unzipping your body; let it drop to the floor. Who is that? Start with that question. Who are you without the body? Perhaps write this down. Who are you? And can you take that feeling and multiply it times 10? What does that feel like? What vibration are you when you multiply you, without the body, times 10. Practice this, this week. It is fun. Make it light. Make it fun! You will feel better, just by doing this process. Think of it as a game.

J: Thank you.

10: Of course.

J: I think it would be fun to dream of that all night.

10: You may do that, and you may live it as well.

J: Yes.

10: Dreaming is a part of your consciousness; it is your sub-consciousness. You're relaxed when you sleep, and you may choose to be equally relaxed when you are awake. At some point, you will know no difference.

J: Thank you again.

10: Always. We are trying to open Michelle's eyes. We wish to look around the room. Michelle is fighting us. Please tell her not to resist. We shall not harm her in any way. We simply hope to use her vehicle to look around the room.

J: Baby, it's okay to let them look around the room.

10: That is enough for now. She may rest. Thank you.

J: Thank you. We'll talk soon.

10: Yes.

CHAPTER 5

Asking the Right Questions

We would most like you to ask a question of us this morning.

Michelle was doing her yoga practice when we posed this to her, and the first thing that came out of her mind was to wonder, "When will it all happen?"

She was not specific, but we laugh at her question—not because it is a poor one, but because it so accurately represents how you all understand time.

Let us make this clear: It is all happening now—*all* of it.

Now, you might wonder where it "all" is. Why "it" hasn't shown up materially in your reality. It is not your reality that needs to change; it's simply your perception. You do not "see" or experience it at this moment simply because you have not learned to tune into the right frequency to match it.

It is all happening right now, at the same exact time.

Time, in your world, is a measurement. Where we lie, there are no measurements, no eking things out into portions so we may meet up somewhere in space. We are everywhere. We think, and that soul appears, in us, as us.

It is all happening at once.

You see time as linear in motion, as a hillside that goes straight up. We do not see it as such. It is more of a whirling ball constantly in motion, much like your planet, only much faster. The reason you do not see life on other planets is either because they are at a higher, faster vibration where you cannot see them with the naked eye, or because they no longer need to step foot on a ground. They no longer require the sustenance and protection that a body has to have. They have moved beyond those necessities required in your dimension.

The ascension process that some of you recognize is simply a matter of moving closer toward who you really are: millions of tiny "balls" in high motion, moving more rapidly when they are fueled by higher thoughts and emotions. Move your cells fast enough, and they appear to disappear, like the blades of a ceiling fan.

If you find yourself impatient with your life story—like you'd like to read ahead to the final chapter—simply imagine what that final chapter might look like, and feel good inside as if it has already happened. Those good feelings will bring the "ending" closer to you, with a magnetic quality that is beyond your current level of understanding. Think, feel, draw it to you. Make it simple.

Then again, do you really want to skip ahead to your ending? Perhaps not yet. Perhaps you have an inkling of your life pre-birth, a time when you chose this adventure and particular life story to add to your list of intrinsic values: Love, courage, compassion, strength, resilience, hope, passion, service, kindness.

So instead of asking, "When is it all going to happen?" Why not ask, "Where am I now, in relation to these values?"

"What can I do in this moment that will allow those values to be the real Truth of what I exhibit?"

You see, it is all about asking the right question. When you start to feel a sense of impatience looming, perhaps look at it from the lens of impending manifestation—a sort of building up of energy that is ready to release into form. Allow any feelings of excitement to build. This should be an enjoyable process and one worth doing. For when you finally do see it materialize into form, it is within your human nature to ask, "What's next?"

When Michelle sees clients in her office, they often ask this very question. Using her refined sense of intuition, Michelle relays what she sees for them in relationship to where their energy is at that moment. If the client were to speed up their energy, they would see what she sees much more rapidly. Conversely, if they are afraid of what she sees for the changes it might bring, they could very well block that vision and keep it from happening soon, if at all. Additionally, that person may decide that's not what they want at all! In which case, they can alter their path by thinking thoughts that manipulate their energy flow to bring about a new desired result.

It is all energy. Rather than stew in impatience, why not get more in touch with your energy levels and practice raising them? One of the easiest ways of doing this is by using your words. Parents often say just this to frustrated toddlers: "Use your words," as words have meaning and make manifest thought into form.

Whenever you wish to raise your energy levels, simply recite the word *rise* 10 times. With each time you pronounce the word, feel your life force awakening and rising up to the command. It may feel like your body tingles. You may feel a temperature change, or a feeling not unlike an alcohol "buzz." It is a higher vibration change that will make you feel light, perhaps even slightly dizzy. Your body will soon adjust to this higher level as you allow it and practice it daily. Even such slight adjustments to your vibration on a regular basis will yield tremendous results!

Pass this information on to like-minded friends and family who are open to such ideas, and collectively you will begin to raise energy levels across your planet. Someday, you may not even need to feed off your planet any longer, and Earth, she may rest in peace.

SUCCESS

Success is maintaining a high vibrating state while living your life.

This state is not altered by varying circumstances, as there is a surety in who you truly are and what you are led to do through your feelings of excitement and enthusiasm.

Let Love be your guide, and you shall never falter.

When success is achieved, more success is derived. All you need is a little bit of progress to beget more feelings of success, which equate to more materializations of success, and so forth. You just have to do your part in getting the ball rolling, simply by seeing the successes that are already yours.

Did you wake up this morning? We would call that a win. Did you find a nice thought inside your head when you got up? That's a success. Were you able to prepare a light meal? Success. Do you see the direction we are going? This does not have to be huge. Not at all. Begin by witnessing all the small successes already present in your life, and you are sure to see more.

Once the ball is moving, and you are feeling and engaging with this new momentum, you will likely find yourself giddy with excitement. This is good—very good! You might find yourself surpassing all the dreams and goals you set out for yourself, and then ask, "Now what?" Right now, sit down and ask yourself how it might feel if you were to check off all those things and experiences on your list? You know—-your list. You must keep one. We know you do.

Now sit and bask into something beyond that list—you do not have to conceptualize what that might be, just bathe in the knowing that there is so much more.

Then amplify. Times 10.

If you want, amplify again times 10, until your body just can't take it anymore. When you've reached the pinnacle of your excitement level for the day, allow some time for your body to adjust. Your soul already knows it's a part of Spirit. Your body vehicle may take some time catching up, and that is okay.

Alternatively, it may not. The cells inside your body may leap with joy that your mind is finally grasping what it is capable of! Right now, the very nucleus of each cell inside your body is vibrating and rotating more rapidly than ever before. Even a small increase daily in your cells' rpm will yield better health and vitality, and evidential success in your ever-changing life story.

You may have thought things out with your angels and guides pre-birth, but you can alter and edit the course of your life script as you go along. You've had this power always. You are just waking up to the magnitude of this power.

And when you get to the way station, now you know. You know that you've achieved the levels of success that you had always dreamed of throughout thousands of lifetimes, and so you may choose a different path to a lighter reality now—toward us.

Or, you may begin to doubt where this is all headed. You may tell yourself you are not worthy, because your parents or bosses or friends said so. You may see signs of success and sabotage yourself because your alleged friends feel jealousy, so you dumb yourself down in an attempt to placate what you deem "the masses."

The Truth is, you are part of the great masses of those who seek a higher reality—one that does not involve criticism, violence, or destruction. There are more of you than you know, more that inhabit your entire galaxy and beyond. There are indeed 10 x 10 x 10 souls and more who were once in your shoes and graduated and spiritual evolved to new heights just so they could assist you in going forward.

Don't you feel so loved?

When you doubt your worth as a soul who is part of the great Spirit that encompasses worlds, you are lessening your vibration. And just as the ball rolls up, it can just as rapidly roll down the hill.

Don't do that.

Why would you? Doubting your worth causes suffering, and suffering causes pain. We are here primarily to share with you that there is an easy path toward peace, and it involves having faith. Faith is the key. Faith is trust in something more, something greater, than your daily existence.

Flow

We promised that Eudicine would share some words on the concept of flow and surrender, and we find it appropriate here, as it pertains to success and asking the right questions.

When you ask the right question and follow your inner guidance, life attains a flow that most effortlessly leads to success. Others may offer differing ways to success than your own, and you may contemplate if their ways feel good to you or not, and choose accordingly. Remember that our definition of success is maintaining your highest vibration available at any given time. And so, if their suggestion maintains or even raises your vibrational level, you might say yes.

We would like to give as an example the structure of this book. We led Michelle toward a literary agent who might best serve our needs of getting our message out to as many of you as possible. The agent had served past recipients of nonphysical energy, and so, she matched the frequency of our desire.

This agent requested a change in structure of our book, allowing for the audio sessions we recorded through Michelle to be transcribed and added to the writings. We thought that would be a good idea, and so when Jodah asked the right question, we agreed because it was of like mind.

It is all the same information we are giving, just in differing ways in order to reach various levels of frequency. Wherever it is you are standing right now is okay. We are just here to point you toward the next level of your existence. There is always a next step. Even where we are, there are billions of levels of dimensions in time and space. They all consist in variables of 10.

And so, you may be at 10, but if you multiply times 10, you will be at a 100. And if you multiply 100x10 ... we will not do the math for you, but you see how quickly you can rise if you choose.

In your daily life, rather than resisting what another has to offer, consider how it makes you feel, and act accordingly. How does it feel to flow through life rather than fight it? How might it feel to surrender your beliefs on how things should be, and soften them into a mild wondering of how things might be if you try something new? Creativity starts from this space, and creativity is the source of all lifetimes.

Think of all the people who share your planetary existence as co-creators of a majestic tapestry. Each must do their part. Heed your vibration in your corner of the tapestry, and surrender to the greater picture.

This idea of flow becomes easier if you start your day with the right attitude. Attitude is simply a barometer of your current emotions, and the beauty of it is, you can choose another one! If you rise in the morning feeling the heaviness of your body, put your focus on the comfort of your bed, or the fact that you have fingers or toes. Gratitude and appreciation are words that have been bandied about a great deal—and yet, we'd like you to feel the space behind those words and truly embody them. They should not ebb, but be in a constant state of flow. We promise: if you begin by flowing out gratitude and appreciation at the early onset of your day, you will enjoy magnificent experiences. You are here to enjoy magnificent experiences. That is the whole point.

BEAUTY

There is so much beauty all around you, and yet you do not see.

Take a look around you. If you would just open your eyes and gaze upon the wonderment that is your reality, it would take your breath away.

And look for more than just a few seconds. Your word *gaze* implies a longer look. Rather than flitting about like a butterfly, why not really see into your surroundings? Even when you go for a walk, it is often with a hurried gait that doesn't stop to take the time to take in the flowers and trees.

The next time you find yourself on a walk (not a run—that's simply too fast for what we are asking you to do), please stop every few steps to gaze upon what is in front of you. If you are walking with another, take the time to look at them and see the beauty of their individuality. If you are with a beloved dog, have them sit—perhaps on a bench if one is available—and as you pet their fur, take in the softness or coarseness of it, and maybe look into the depth of their eyes.

Pause.

Repeat this process: walking, then pausing and gazing in wonderment. Then amplify those feelings times 10. We know we've mentioned this before, but we want you to really do this and not make excuses about how you don't have enough time. You have all the time in the world. Carve out some *space* in your schedule to practice the tools we are giving you, and if you don't feel amazing by the end of the experiment, then you simply aren't ready to ascend to the next dimension of living.

Q: But what about my JOB?

We hear this question all the time, and so we thought we'd answer it to the best of your ability to hear it.

If your j-o-b is taking up so much of your daily routine, as well as lowering your vibration to unsatisfactory levels, why do you keep doing it?

Is it to put a roof over your head? What if you might simplify to a smaller home? Is it to feed the body vehicle? What if you could grow your own fruits and vegetables?

Or is there another way of life which might make your heart sing? One in which you wake excited to get started, and the hours just flow on by because you are thrilled to do this practice. It helps humanity in some way, and makes enough of your money to give you the feelings of freedom, which are indeed the Truth of who you are intrinsically.

We'd like to emphasize this: You ARE free already.

Affirm this now: I am free.

What does freedom feel and look like to you? Take a few moments now to contemplate this word, and perhaps jot down some experiences you might have if you felt your freedom.

WANDERING

Now that you know your innate sense of freedom, you may build on this by practicing the lost art of wandering.

The reason so many of you enjoy travelling to new locales is because when you are on vacation, you are not worrying about your j-o-b or any other responsibilities.

Now some of you may still plan out your vacation to the point of making it a chore, and we would hope that you can distance yourself from this fruitless activity. However, many more of you will allow yourself to simply discover the freedom of not holding to an agenda and discovering new places and peoples.

You don't have to go on vacation to do this. Many of you gobble up many, many precious hours of your daily schedule collecting enough vacation time in an effort to save up and spend copious amounts of dollars on extravagant vacation places, just in an effort to "relax."

That time may be better spent in walking, gazing, and meditation. You may wander from wherever you are at! Perhaps start by taking a long break, packing your lunch, and wander away from your worksite into an adjacent neighborhood. Notice the similarities and differences of the yards, the differing ways people choose to decorate the fronts of their homes.

You can also visit a neighboring town and go into a store you've never gone to before, just to look around and maybe chat with the staff. Find a new trail if you live near open land, or sit in the midst of a group of people in a park or market square.

In essence, do the things you might save up to do on a vacation from where you are. And then, when you do find yourself longing to be in a differing section of your world, do those same activities there, and you will amplify your enjoyment! The "trick" is to amplify existing feelings of joy and excitement.

We, as non-physical creatures, watch with amazement your wanderings. We live vicariously through your new discoveries of the physical planet around you—for we are beyond that stage in our soul's evolution—and yet we marvel at its beauty, just as you do.

When we see the beauty of the tree, we also recognize that in Truth, we *are* the tree. There is no separation.

Yet it is fun to see you observe the tree as outside of you, as your progress in your knowing of a higher reality.

Q&A - LOVE IS, IN TRUTH, THE ABSENCE OF ALL JUDGMENT

10: Good Evening.

J: Hello.

10: Hello. I would like to speak to you tonight as one who is known as Theras. I am—I have been—male more times than female. Therefore, I have a different energy than many in the group. I would like to come forward tonight to speak of Love, in all of its various forms. Is that something you would like to discuss?

J: I would love to. Thank you.

10: You said "love." You are all concerned with finding one great love, yes? And we are all here to tell you that you are all magnets of Love, drawn to each other by virtue of your vibration. You are all made out of pure Love, and it is your mission to find out who you truly are. There is no need to find one great love. That is only a form of separation. Your mission is to find the Love that is you, that is inside of you, that *is* you. It's not even inside of you, it IS you. Again, when you traject forward out of body you realize the purity of what you are made of. You wander around this world, drawn to and repelled by each other, based upon your vibration. That is all.

You are like puzzle pieces. Sometimes you get attached, and you get stuck if you're in the wrong space. If it is the right space, you simply move on when you are ready, when you have learned the lesson. And some will learn to stay together and magnify their Love. It's all a choice. Do you have a question for me?

J: I don't think I do yet.

10: Some would ask of gender. And we would like to say, of course, it makes no difference. When you are out of body, you no longer have a gender. You no longer have a race. There is nothing to separate you—no skin, no body—only your soul, which knows no body parts. You separating into various "themes" is ridiculous, if I might say so. Love transcends all of those boundaries, and when you traject out of the recycling, you will know Love at a deeper level.

Q: So the main reason for loving each other is to understand the Love that we're made of?

A: You are to understand the Love first. When you are drawn toward each other, it is simply a matter of learning lessons, either together or apart. When you split up, you learn just as much as you do when you stay together, no? Therefore, it is not a judgment when people leave each other. And when they stay, it is very enjoyable as well. It is not "bad" or "good." There is no judgment on the other side, as well as beyond in the space where we reside. We all gather together in Love, and it is a choice occasion every day. Every day we experience Love, and we amplify Love. When you feel Love, it is important to multiply it times the power of 10, as we have taught you, and we will continue to teach you again and again. When two come together and they amplify the Love together, it is amplified times one hundred. And when three come together, or more, it is amplified even more into the power of 10.

The more of you that Love and come together in Love, the more you will feel your vibration rise together. Therefore, if you find yourself in a loving relationship together, it is important to gather together with others of a like mind and vibration. Together, you will know the Truth, and you will raise it to new levels.

I have a story for you. I had a wife many, many lives ago, and she taught many of the things that I am passing on to you today. And now together we are one being, one soul. She no longer needs to teach me as we are one, as in Truth we all are. I only choose to step out today in order to share with you this Truth, as part of the collective whole. She was my guiding force, and you may have the opportunity to share your life with such a desirous occasion.

We know you have questions. They are there, and we wish for you to respond.

J: Everything that you say resonates inside me as the reason for true love, of all Love. And I am having— the questions are not coming forward to my mind because it all sounds perfect. I don't feel conflict or curiosity in what you say because it just feels right.

10: Perhaps it would be good at this time to discuss the nature of Love. And to define what it is. It is in Truth the absence of all judgment. When you point the finger and blame each other, that is the opposite of Love. You must catch yourself before you do this, and know that that is not Love. Change it before it grabs hold and becomes something bigger.

The nature of Love is sweetness. It is not bitterness. It is not resentment. All of those are lower vibrating emotions. Love is the highest there is, and that is all there is. In Truth, that is what fills the Universe. It is not oxygen or helium or any of your gases, it is all Love. If you were to traject yourself into the Universe—without being in our space and still having a body—you wouldn't be able to breathe, because you wouldn't be able to adjust to that sense of Love. That's all there is. You must be beyond the body in order to breathe it and drink it in, because in Truth you are one with it. And it only expands. As space expands; so does Love. It is like bread in an oven. It keeps growing.

All you need to do to attract Love is to be. That is all. You, on this planet, are like magnets drawn to each other. That is all. You make it so complicated.

J: Yes, we do.

10: When you Love another, you care for another as you would yourself. Selfishness begets greed, and begets more lower-vibrating emotions. Care for one another. Take care of each other. Care if someone is hungry or thirsty. Take care of each other.

Q: Where is the balance between caring for each other and—when more and more people's vibration rises and there is the separation to the lower vibrations—where is that balance between caring and letting go?

A: That is a very good question. You care for each other when you Love one another. Those who drift away—you care for them, but you must Love them enough to let them go their own way. They will sink, and they will either rise up to join you, or they will sink into the lower and the lower vibrations. Love those that you feel Love toward and who Love you. You'll know the difference. There is a different feeling. Your magnets will draw each other toward the right people and energies and vibratory consistencies that will draw you together in groups, just like The Power of 10 is together because we are all of a like vibration. We all project different aspects of the Divine consciousness. However, so do you—just at a lower level.

And by lower, we don't mean to undermine your efforts. You are doing the best you can at this moment in your time. That is all that is expected of you. And if you wish to grow exponentially, you Love times the power of 10. And when you are feeling Love, when you are feeling joy and peace and understanding and compassion, you grow those feelings. It can be done with one another. Hold each other's hands and stare into each other's eyes. And amplify the level of your Love.

That is the next tool that I will give to you. My wife in that time period and I did this, and it was a very valuable tool that I hope to share with you. Have the courage to open up and be with one another, and look into each other's eyes—and go deeper until you feel as if you are one soul, because in Truth, you are.

J: I like that idea.

Q: So the groups that vibrate on similar levels will come together in each group of people—each group of souls will continue to help each other, not in a competitive way, but each person of a certain level can most be helped by people that are just a little above their level vibrationally? As opposed to someone who is a very high vibration?

A: Those who are vibrating at a similar level will gather together. Whether it is slightly higher or slightly lower does not matter. You will all be drawn to each other. That power will be magnified. If it is much lower, you will soon not even notice it exists, because it is out of your vibration. It is as if, Michelle, when she walks her dog in the morning, and she walks by what you call the "barky" dogs, and she has the dog ignore the other barky dogs for a treat. And the dog has learned to ignore the barky dogs because they are at a different vibration from where she is at, and she is expecting a great reward. The same is true for how you Love each other. There is great reward when you come together, and Love and care for each other, and soon you will not even hear the barky dogs.

It is not that you are not caring for them; you will not even notice their existence, and they will not know yours. They are separating out. And soon, if they are going to know oneness, they will switch paths, and if they are not, then they will destroy themselves. Neither is your concern. It is for them to learn to continue on the recycling path of coming back to earth again and again, until they learn, and learn how to traject far out of that cycle. It is not "bad." Please do not see it as such. It is the most loving thing you can do: to Love yourself and those around you who share the same vibration. When you do, you lift up both of your vibrations, and you are an example to the world. They may choose to follow your example, or they may choose to recycle back on earth. All of it is a choice.

Q: Was there a recycling on the planet Mars, or is that something that's coming in our linear future?

A: There are already beings on Mars. They are of a different consistency. You don't notice them because they are a completely different vibration with different needs. And just like your dog Sunny does not notice the barky dogs, you do not notice those on Mars. They are a completely different vibration.

J: Cool.

10: We would like to add that for the most part they are of a lower vibration. Many of you would think they are higher, but we see them as a lower vibration, that you have achieved a greater—how shall we say—a wisdom over ... and in much the same way, your humans will drop to where you no longer even notice their existence. There are beings all over on many planets. Why would there not be?

J: Good question. (laughs)

10: They are simply not like you. They are not blue, either.

J: (Laughs) That makes perfect sense then, in what you're saying about where humans at higher and lower vibrations will no longer be aware of each other's presence. There are other beings at higher and lower vibrations. It sounds like the same thing.

10: It is all a matter of your spiritual evolutionary cycle. That is all.

J: That makes more sense than blue Martians.

10: It does. Do you have more questions for us?

J: I don't think I do right now. I need to explore this idea of Love ...

10: After you get to the number 10 session, you can ask someone to join into your sessions whom you trust a great deal. They may be able to add more questions of an outside influence. But first, you must get used to the vibratory conditions between Michelle and all of us before you share it with the outside world. It is very important. We are here to teach, and in order to teach, it is a call-and-response situation.

Take all the time you need. If you do not have questions, do not force them to come, because remember, there is no force. Either the questions arise in the moment or not at all, and that is okay. We have all the time in the world because, in Truth, there is no time.

J: Okay.

Q: Is there something that Michelle can do to allow the vibration to sit with her the best?

A: That is why we allow for at least 10 sessions. She will get used to it in time. Everyone who receives us goes through the same process. And different aspects of The Power of 10 will react with her body differently as they learn to utilize her mouth movements and her body. And she needs to be in a receptive position. She will only allow this through meditation and relaxation techniques, which she knows well of.

Q: Does this soreness that she feels in her jaw and her legs, is that because of resistance?

A: It is from another energy manipulating her body. In time, she will get used to this. It is a temporary resistance.

At any time, if she chooses to say no to us she can as well; it is all her choice. We come to you both voluntarily. Our mission is a peaceful one: to raise the vibration of those on your planet who wish to do so, to traject to a higher place beyond the recycling, and to reach a level that we are at, that is of pure Love and joy and bliss and peace and happiness—that is all. There is absolutely nothing to fear. Remind Michelle of this fact.

J: Okay. We enjoy speaking with you immensely.

10: Thank you for this opportunity.

J: Thank you.

CHAPTER 6

World Affairs

We just encouraged Michelle to take a bath.

She was doing some yoga, and she was clearing her mind in anticipation of receiving our words, and we found her mind cloudy from the previous day's events and other people's energy and affairs.

We are so happy Michelle followed our suggestion, and as she relaxed in warm waters with salts, she cleansed her auric energy fields, as well as readied the canvas of her mind to receive us.

You would do well to immerse yourself on occasion in water. Whether it is in a small body of water, such as a bath or hot tub, or larger waters such as lakes, rivers, and oceans, it is soothing to your soul on so many levels, and across many layers of dimensions, as well. Bet you never thought of that last part!

Other people's affairs are not yours.

We will repeat this for you, because it is an essential concept for you to grasp before you can move on. *Other people's affairs are not yours.* And you may think you have this down intellectually, but until you know it with all of your being, you will not thrive. When your energy field is murky, you are like a muddy pond. Focus on your own soul's path, and your pond will become clear like a mountain lake.

This includes, of course, your politics. We see you getting all irate about the peoples you put at the top to make decisions and rules about the way you should live. As long as you are not hurting anyone, you get to live life your own way. Why would you do anything else?

To lower your energy field by focusing on what someone can or cannot do for you is just foolish. When you do this, you are acting more like a preschooler than a kindergartner, and as we've said before, we are here to help you graduate into higher states of being.

You might ask, "But what about the wars?"

What about the wars? Ask yourself your true feelings about wars across the world, not just in your own neighborhood. If everyone on your planet spent some time exploring their belief systems and exorcised any violent thoughts toward others, war would end as you know it.

You might be pointing your fingers at your politicians right now.

Anytime you give your expansive powers over to another you lose. You create this reality in each moment. Tune into your current vibration, amplify, then multiply some more. Those in your midst will feel your expansiveness, and their proximity alone may be enough to raise their own consciousness. When this expands enough, someone is bound to be around a politician. Once that politician (that you put in charge) is around enough higher vibrational politicians who FEEL the enhanced vibration of the people in her or his midst, they cannot help but RISE. And rise is what we aim to do, yes?

What else can you do in this moment to rise? We've been asked to make it simple for you, and we shall comply with this request. You're probably not going to like this tool either, so you may decide whether you wish to play along or not. If we told you your world could achieve peace within your lifetime, would you do what we ask?

This involves your closet. We want you to clean it all out.

Yes, you heard us, and yes, we know there are other teachers who compare the clutter of your closets to the clutter of your minds. And we'd like to commend those teachers for their teachings. So much of life is an allegory, you see. Clear house, clear body, clear closet, clear mind.

If you cannot carve the space out you need to complete this task, then perhaps throw out one item you no longer need or use. Donate it so that it may circulate to someone who needs it. Notice how you feel as you rid yourself of this unnecessary item.

If you amplify this feeling far enough, that is how you might feel if there were no more wars.

From our perspective, you have needed your wars throughout time to learn your lessons, to understand compassion and the knowledge that you are all one. You fight over property like kindergarteners might fight over crayons, and in time, you will help each other more often than killing each other. It is possible, and we see it as coming true for you.

Where we are, of course, there is no need for war, because there are no bodies to kill or properties to steal. WE—and YOU—are all pure states of consciousness. When you can truly know for yourself this Truth, you will be free of fear. And being free of fear equates peace, yes?

Q&A - Remember, it is all an illusion

10: Good afternoon.

J: Hello.

10: How are you this day?

J: Happy to be talking to you.

10: We are happy as well.

J: I listened to the recordings from the last two times and came up with many follow-up questions.

10: That is good. We enjoy your questions. Proceed.

Q: I sometimes find that the balance between the human daily experience is in contrast to living a spiritually-centered life. Do you have any advice for finding balance in those two?

A: Your human experience, as you call it, is all an illusion. The Divine is present in every moment of your existence. If you can enter through this moment in time, in the present moment, and make every single act a sacred one, you may enjoy your time here immensely. However, as we have stated before, when the time is right, and you choose to leave this body and choose to traject into space, perhaps you may choose the next time to learn without suffering. Suffering and contrast is the nature of your human existence, and your daily life—as you call it—is a great deal of your suffering. What is the lesson that you choose to learn from this daily existence at this moment in time?

J: That's a really good question that I don't know the answer to yet.

10: And that is okay. You may sit with the question, and in meditation the answers will come. In the meantime, remember it is all an illusion. It is all of your making.

Q: How did this concept of learning through contrast and suffering start?

A: You are all, as human beings, like babies. You are learning as babies do. You are standing up and stumbling as you learn to walk. Learning through suffering is the same way. You must learn through contrast before you choose some different way of learning. It is time for you—you've had many, many hundreds of thousands of cycles—many of you. Not all. Your babies will choose to continue until they are ready to graduate. However, many of you are ready to graduate and are simply resisting that graduation, thinking that there are more creature pleasures here. That is not the Truth of who you are. The Truth of who you are is much wider and expansive than you have any understanding of. When you leave this existence and unzip your body to reveal the Truth of who you are, you will know so much more. But you, for now, have chosen to learn through contrast, because you are babies in the infinity of this life, as we know it. Do you understand?

J: I do. That's amazing. That makes sense.

10: It is all part of your unfolding and evolution.

Q: And so, when you said we were never supposed to repeat this recycling process so many times, what you're saying is we've just—even our souls have gotten used to the recycling process ... that we are resisting the higher levels?

A: It is becoming like a bad habit. You get to the way station, and you dive right back in before any learning takes place. You think there's more of an adventure down here than it is beyond this existence, because you don't know any better. But we are here to tell you—is that for many of you—there is an alternative choice. And when you get to the way station, you can choose to connect with like-minded frequencies, with other souls who share your frequency.

You may do that now. You may come together in a vibratory gathering and amplify your energies. If you get one thing from these sessions, it is that you can multiply your energies and traject beyond—so much further beyond than what you are currently existing. It is all a choice.

Reincarnation is a beautiful thing—and there are those of you who do not even believe in that—and it is the Truth of how you learn at this point in time. However, there is a place beyond reincarnation, just as there is a place beyond what you call "heaven."

Heaven is not a house.

It is a dimensional space. There are millions of dimensions beyond what your small brain can conceive, and we do not mean this as an insult.

Again, you are simply at a certain point in your spiritual unfoldment. We hope these sessions can help you expand your consciousness. That is why are here.

J: It's certainly expanding my consciousness.

10: That is good. You are representative, Jodah, of many.

Q: Why is our human ego so resistant to spirituality?

A: Ego believes that it is the death of itself. When the soul chooses the Truth of who it is, which is spirituality, it is space, it is all there is, it is freedom. Ego says it is your individual, small self—why would you choose that? It is a part of your process. That is all. It is part of the unfoldment to move beyond this limited sense of self. You are so much more than that. When you are ready to give up the ego, you will give it up just as you give up your body. Some people will not give it up until they do give up the body. Then they realize they are not the ego.

All this striving for your earthly successes is all just play. You take it so seriously. It is nothing. It is just a game. It is the same kind of learning games you play in preschool. It is as if you are playing with puzzles.

You are more than that. Know that. Affirm that daily. Play the game, as we showed you: the tool of unzipping your body and watching it drop to the floor as if it is a pile of clothes. Underneath that is your soul, which is part of the Spirit, which is a part of all that is. You are energy. Many of you know this. Many of your scientists know this, and they are the most resistant of them all.

Q: That falls into another question—what we call the emptiness of the Universe. Our scientists are only looking for what we can scientifically prove and measure. And since Love, as you said, is what the Universe is filled with—and Love is the highest vibration—we won't find that until we match that vibration, will we?

A: You cannot find Love under a microscope. All the empty space you see is full and vibrating and teeming with Life. You simply need to look with different eyes. You will experience it. You are looking in the wrong place. Look inside your heart for now. That should be enough.

Q: When you talked about spirit guides, you mentioned that it was their hope that the person who they are helping—it is their hope that they ask for help out loud. And so, I'm wondering what the difference is between saying something out loud and consciously thinking the same thought.

A: It is a violation to impede in a person's thoughts. That is their privacy inside of their head. Once you leave the body, or traject beyond it where we reside, it is all exposed. There are no private thoughts. It is different; it is beyond where you currently are. In order to help you achieve this, you must either say it aloud or write it down. You must put it in form for us to know that it is okay, and we have permission to help you.

It is not our job to get in the way of your learning; that would impede your process. We are there simply to guide the way, to give you signs, to talk to you, and have you listen if you choose. We are available for this at all times, but many of you use your left brain to turn it off and say it doesn't exist—that we are only ghosts or figments of your imagination. Why would you resist something that is being given to you, which is a gift?

You may choose that, and you will not move beyond, and that is okay as well. However, there are many, many teachers in many dimensions that are waiting to help you because you are babies. We like babies.

J: We like babies down here, too.

Q: You mentioned ghosts. When Michelle does her work she calls them earthbound spirits who seem to be confused about going on to the way station. What is the vibration of those souls?

10:   It is all a continuum of vibration. You have those of you who are here on earth, who are vibrating at the densest level. You pass away and leave your bodies, and sometimes you are still so focused on earthly activities that you don't even know there is a way station or that you can choose to heal or come back. Those are the souls that Michelle rightly coaches into the other side.

It is the same with those in the way station. They are still so focused on coming back that they don't know that there is an alternative existence that they can traject to. It is not up to us to point that direction. It is up to them to live enough lives till they realize when they leave the body that they can choose more.

It is all a continuum.

Once you have lived enough lifetimes, and you vibrate higher and higher with all the lessons— once you start learning and remembering all the lessons from your many lifetimes of existence— when you wake up, you will traject to where we are. When the greater masses come to you and listen to these messages, they will know that there is an even higher choice. Therefore, as Michelle points the way for earthbound ghosts to go into the way station, there will now be an even higher choice to go from the way station—and multiply it times 10 to be in the free place where we are—of bliss and joy and peace and happiness—and multiply it again times 10, and times 10 again, until the Universe expands with bliss and joy. That is how it expands.

Q: Do animal spirits recycle the same way that humans do, and vice versa? Or do they come back as humans sometimes and animals sometimes?

A: They tend to go back and forth. Animals, by and by, are here to comfort us and lead the way to higher vibratory states. They are simply happy being who they are. They do not need to traject. They are vibrating at a very high level just being where they are at. Have you ever noticed that animals are always happy? If they are not, it is because you are using violence against them. Most of the time, if they act out, it is just out of protection. If they choose, they can stay up at the way station with your deceased loved ones to give them comfort as well. Michelle sees them all the time at the way station with their loved ones. Their energy, though, does not traject to the place where we are at. That is not a bad thing. If they choose to become human, and then traject beyond form, then that is one way that they may do so. But it is not the common one. Think about it—if you are a happy cat, why would you come back into a human existence?

J: That's what I was just thinking. Our cats are pretty happy.

10: Yes.

J: As long as we feed them.

10: All the animals are.

J: You said it is a violation to read our thoughts. So when you're using examples, say of walking the dog—that example comes from watching her actions and not ... well obviously, that example would be her actions. Scratch that.

10: Of what example are you speaking of?

J: I was speaking of the example of the dog ignoring the barky dogs for the treat, knowing that certain vibrations will just not even appear once we are vibrating higher—we just won't be able to see the lower vibrations.

10: Yes, that is simply a demonstration that we use—a story, if you will. All the great leaders and masters of your day spoke in stories and metaphors and similes, as you call them. Your dog, Sunshine, walking past the barky dogs and ignoring them, knowing that there would be a greater reward, is simply an example of how you may choose to behave in similar situations. When a lower vibration presents itself, you know the greater reward lies in simply ignoring it and keeping your walk.

J: That is a perfect example.

10: That is how you do it. And then when you are feeling higher vibration, and you have successfully passed those barky dogs, as you call them, then you can take that feeling and you can amplify it. Find a similar frequency of a friend, or a partner, or a spouse, or whoever is near you, and look into their eyes and choose to see the whole entire Universal creation. Know that you are both of that, and multiply it times 10 x 10 x 10 ... and see how you feel. Use the word rise to lift you higher. Have you been practicing the tools that we gave you?

J: We've been practicing rise, and we practiced looking into each other's eyes only once, which is not enough, because it was wonderful.

10: How did it make you feel?

J: Amazing.

10: Take the amazing feeling, and multiply it times 10 today.

J: Okay.

10: You may do that in your quieter moments. It does not take a lot of what you call "time." Remember that. And when you carve out another section of time, you may do it at will. It is simply a tool we give to you to feel better and better and better—to climb the scales of your vibration, to reach a place that feels so good that when you choose to leave this body and this lifetime, you will say, "Hey, this vibratory state feels amazing," as you call it. And you will multiply it times 10, and you will seek out other vibrations, and you will all congregate. And then you may choose to help others, or you may just choose to float around and feel amazing.

Q: Are each one of you souls that have recycled on earth as humans only? Or have some or all of you spent lifetimes on other planets and in other dimensions before you got to where you are now?

A: All of us have been through your particular human forms many times, as we have said before. Once you traject to another dimension, you don't need a body. Why do you think you have not discovered other bodies on other planets? That is just unique to *your* planet with its gases and waters and food supply, and when you traject beyond it, there are many, many life forms, and all of them are non-physical.

Look out in your telescopes. You do not see bodies. They no longer need that. Space is teeming with millions, and billions—and numbers that you cannot even imagine—of non-physical entities. *Believe*, because how many of your people have already died and come back many, many times?

That is billions upon billions of souls that fill up the Universe, that populate the cosmos. You just do not see them with your naked eye. You do not have telescopes that can handle that level of vibratory speed, as of yet. Those who *do* see, you mock them, because those are the bringers of the Light. They are the teachers and the guideposts that will lead the way.

Soon, very soon, there will be more of you, and with each generation you will become more and more aware. And as more people learn of their choices beyond the way station, of their choices to project their vibration, you will join the masses of us who exist in a state beyond life and death, as you currently experience it—a space that is beyond suffering.

You came here because you wanted to learn, and it is a valuable resource. But there is so much more beyond this particular time and space. Look to your children. They are now being born vibrating at a naturally higher state. With each level of existence, and your acceptance of them, they will know the Truth. Look into your children's eyes. It is a wide and vast cosmos inside of there.

When they ask you questions, as children often do, do not shut them down, either. Welcome the questions, and if you don't know the answers, then tell them so. Sit with it, and soon you will come to those answers together. Do not let your outer society and other people tell you how to think. Look for the answers inside of you—inside of Source Energy. Together with your children, you can teach them how to raise their vibration. There is nothing more valuable than to teach your children this.

J: Okay.

10: Michelle has a daughter who is a teenager, yes?

J: Yes.

10: And if you teach her to walk past the barky dogs, as you teach your dog, that would be a very valuable tool, don't you think? There are many barky dogs in middle school. There are other entities in children who are in the way of her greater learning. She can choose either to sink lower to their lower vibration, or she can rise above and know the true reward of knowing the Truth of who she is.

J: Michelle wanted me to ask you about her path as a medium, and the work that she's doing, and if you have any guidance on things she can do to go in the right direction.

10: Michelle's ability to hold space for us is simply an evolutionary step in her own process as a medium. Part of the reason we chose her is her ability to clear out her ego and be able to let in Spirit. She did not expect us, and it is her choice if she still wants to connect people with their loved ones in the way station. It is still her choice if she wants to help people remember their past lives; it is valuable to remember the learning and the lessons from past lives in order for those same people to traject eventually when the time is right.

And, as we have said before, when you have collected 10 of these recordings, you may put them on your social media, and the right people will come to you. Eventually, Michelle may feel so good at being the channel for our messages that she no longer needs to do her other work, but that is always a choice. We are very grateful to her for lending her body vehicle to us so that we may have a voice.

She will benefit greatly from these messages as well. And she will benefit greatly from the higher vibratory state that comes to her body by virtue of allowing us to speak through her.

J: Cool.

10: The work she is doing currently is very valuable in that it helps people heal from their alleged loss of other people that are in the way station. And she discusses the means of coming back again to learn more lessons—that this is not a one-shot deal. However, there is more to teach. Eventually, she can tell them with great certainty that there is another choice. And that is to traject beyond and to multiply as we have suggested. For now, there is great healing going on. There is always also great resistance; with great healing co-exists great resistance. Eventually, they will push beyond into the other side—or not. That is not up to Michelle. She is only there to present the messages. It is up to each individual whether they choose to wake up or not. When a person dies, they are indeed in a higher vibratory state; as we have said before, it is all in levels. It is gradual. And therefore, there is some learning that happens by connecting with spirits in the way station. It is simply awareness, and having each person remember that they are multi-dimensional creatures.

J: Ok. I think those are all my questions for today.

10: They are good questions. You will think of more. As you do, call on us when you may. We have enjoyed this session greatly. And there is great Love for you both. Thank you.

J: Thank you.

CHAPTER 7

Intuition and Dreams

We gave Michelle a dream last night, one in which she awoke feeling more clarity about her purpose and our mission.

We were surrounding her in a spa-like environment, giving her a soothing and relaxing facial. We were, in fact, elevating her vibration as she had allowed certain environmental conditions to recently affect her levels, and we wished to communicate more messages through her.

And so, when she awoke, she looked up the meaning of her dream, and read that the facial represented her façade and what she allowed other people to see or know about her.

While we do not wish to be intrusive into Michelle's own life story, we are "in her head" so to speak, while we write to all of you. And when Michelle allows us, we speak using her body vehicle to communicate. And while Michelle is a highly intuitive being, so are all of you. She has elevated her vibration to one that meets our own, and has surrendered to the process. Mostly.

Her dream demonstrates that her unconscious is still wrestling with how other people will perceive her when she reveals that she is indeed the body vehicle through which we communicate. Will they think she's crazy? Probably so. Will they try to attack and kill her? Only if she allows her fears from other centuries and different lifetimes to come to the surface.

Do you emanate a victim mentality? Your "façade" is actually a remnant of your aura, your energy field. It is what both attracts and repels people and experiences in your current lifetime, and it can be cleared by your simple loving attention toward it. Michelle's aura is often clouded by several lifetimes of unconscious memory data that, like a computer, often needs to be looked at, then cleaned out.

Her purpose in this lifetime is to be carried out for the final time, so that she may choose to traject to a much higher level where we reside, to guide other souls to their ongoing journeys. While she is carrying that out, she will undertake her own journey, one that she "signed up" for before this particular birth. All her births leading up to this were planned, and she is a fine example of carrying out her soul's highest mission, based on the guidance she receives on a daily basis.

Are you all privy to such guided information? Absolutely. However, many of you cloud your auras by mundane kindergarteny stuff that blocks what you are here for. Michelle has done such things in her youth, and we have helped her process her emotions to reach the state she is in currently, which is one of receptivity and allowance.

Does that mean her ego does not get in the way at times? Of course not. As long as you are in this body vehicle, you have chosen to be an individual spark of the Divine. As long as you maintain this individuality, your spark will waver. When it blends into the greater part of your soul, you will realize no separation or differences. You may come close in this lifetime, but it is at the way station where you will either leave behind your attachments to this entry level of learning, or choose a higher way of being.

WHAT IS INTUITION?

Your intuition is a state of surrender and allowing that occurs when you give your ego a rest, as in meditation. It speaks to you in various ways when you are in a state of flow and do not allow your thoughts to hinder this receptivity. Without resistant thoughts and criticism, your energetic vibration floats to the top, and it is then that you "hear" it, or "see" evidence of it. You "feel" your way into it, knowing the answers, knowing the Truth, understanding your innate state of wisdom and growth.

Some will follow this guidance, and yet still others will follow the others. Neither is "good or bad," as you like to characterize things. They are simply alternate routes. Some paths might take a little longer than others, and yet, there is simply no single, correct way.

How does it feel when you are following your intuition?

Like a river without boulders, like a powerful rush without end. You will feel a motivation and inspiration like no other, and you will magnetically attract the people and experiences lined up for this soul's mission.

And how does it feel when you are not acting on your inner guidance?

It will feel as if your life has no meaning, as if others are in the way of what you are trying so hard to do. Problems occur, sicknesses appear and reappear. You are getting in your very own way, and it will feel disturbing and disruptive.

What if other people ARE getting in the way?

Get out of their way.

What if that is not possible?

It is always possible. There is an array of choices always at your disposal. If you could truly realize this power of yours, you would remain closer to the Truth of you, and you would be more aligned with Spirit and not so impatient for everything to arrive all at once. It would be a pretty boring life story if everything came all at once, and quite honestly, you—in your current level of understanding—would be overwhelmed.

When you leave the body vehicle behind and transcend into the way station, you will feel free, and high, and light! You will enjoy the rapid manifestation of the creature comforts you left behind, and you will enjoy a closer relationship to those you left behind still in their bodies.

And yet, there is a part of you which will know the Truth—that there is something MORE, something beyond the incarnation cycle of learning through suffering and contrast. Turn your gaze away from what you "left behind" when you pass over, and know that at some point, all of that dimension will make its way toward where you are headed.

Conversely, despite manifesting at will, you will know more patience, as you will understand how everything happens at the same "time" anyway. We want to give you another exercise, one that will require your basic knowledge of being in a meditative state. So if you are already not familiar with how to get yourself in that state, please read another book or take a class in this regard, as we would like to take the rest of you beyond your current "set point."

After centering yourself with deep breathing and clearing your mind of chatter, please now sit in a state of utter patience and complete allowing. Perhaps at first you will need to remind yourself of who you really are without a body, and so, practice visualizing yourself "unzipping" your body. And so, you see yourself as an "invisible" soul, with complete patience and understanding and wisdom.

If you "unzip" and still find yourself restless, perhaps you have not gone deep enough. Sit still until your mind is empty and your soul is free, sit (or walk steadily) until you feel what patience feels like to you.

Does it have a color, a texture? Can you define how you feel? If not, can you memorize this feeling?

Good. There you are.

DREAMS

Why do you think you sleep?

We, who no longer have bodies, never sleep. Your bodies need recharging, and when you sleep you are unplugging your active mind from your perceived reality. Waking up after rest is then the very best time for you to begin a ritual of gratitude and appreciation. We understand many of you *know* this, and yet many of you do not follow through and do it. When you do it enough, it will become second nature, and you will no longer have to program yourself to see the wonder of things first thing in the morning.

And when you dream, we speak to you from beyond. Those in the way station give you messages and visit you when the body is parked in neutral, as you are more receptive than you are in wakefulness. Of course those dreams are real, and if you are not receiving them, it simply means you are not letting go of your mind long enough and deep enough to receive the images and impulses we are offering.

If you are not receiving messages, perhaps you may change a few things you practice in your wakefulness to allow more rest and deep renewal. Dreams are an important way for us to connect with you, and for you to connect to a higher state of *You*.

Q&A - It never ends

10: Good evening.

J: Hello.

10: We are pleased to say hello to you.

J: As we were listening to our last recording with you, I thought it was funny that we've been so wrapped up in the "game," as you called it, for the last couple of weeks. It seems very silly now.

10: It is all a reminder, isn't it? It's a game, and you remind yourself every day that it is just a game; an important game for your learning lessons that will evolve your soul and into your Spirit—eventually you will traject as we have talked about so often. But in the beginning it is a game, and it is an important game.

Q: If the ego thinks that anything spiritual is really the death of itself, I was curious: does the ego remain in some form after the human death, and play a part in the soul recycling repeatedly?

A: The ego remains as a very small part of your essence of your soul, so that when you are in the way station and people contact you, such as [through] mediums, then they know who they are. However, that is a small part of who you are, as you recycle again and again and again and again and again ... until you are a much greater being.

When you traject, when you choose to traject as we do, then there is no ego whatsoever. We separate out on occasion to show you different aspects of your humanness, and that is all. The ego no longer is alive, and that is a very good question. It exists and is an important part of your growing, again, just as your "game" is important, your ego is an important part of your humanness and your spiritual growth. And therefore, do *not* discard it— it is a part of who you are; without it you would not learn. Just as without suffering at this point of your evolution, you would not know how to grow. Eventually it will no longer be needed, just as eventually your ego will also no longer be needed.

It is, to use an example, like your appendix. As Michelle lost her appendix because it is no longer needed in her digestive system, eventually your ego will no longer be needed in your evolutionary growth.

J: That makes sense.

10: We think so.

Q: Does The Power of 10 converse with souls that are in the way station? Or do you—I use the word "converse" loosely—but do you communicate with just those at your level, and angels like you spoke of before, and us, right now?

10: It is all a matter of frequency. If a soul has evolved enough to reach it, then they see that it is an option to traject beyond life and death. If they are a young soul, and they have only recently made it to the way station—only one or two times, perhaps— then no, they don't even know we exist, because it is not of the same energetic frequency.

Angels and non-physical beings such as us can converse because we are within similar frequencies of a very high nature. But no, most of the time they don't even know we are here. It is up to them to learn and to grow until they reach a place where they even know we exist.

If you go into life and death many, many, many, many times—OR you perchance choose to take our advice and to amplify your high vibrating emotions such as peace, happiness, and joy, and bliss—then you will find us sooner or later, and perhaps choose to join us beyond the life and death cycle as you know it.

Q: So then, it's not just enough to be aware in this lifetime that we can traject beyond the way station? It's a matter of repeatedly amplifying our vibration—so that when we do choose to leave the human body behind—that it's a possibility that we would remember to match the frequency or to amplify our frequency after our human death in order to get to a higher place where you are?

A: The fact that you are able to converse with us is enough in itself. You are already vibrating at the frequency where you are aware of our existence. And as more of you are drawn to these teachings, you will know without a DOUBT that the very moment you leave your body and move into the way station, that you won't even need to go to the way station. You will BOUNCE, as you say, beyond into our vibratory place, our dimension where there is such peace and joy and happiness, that it is not of your same words. There is no WORD to describe the place where we are from! But the fact that you are even here and know that this is an option, then when you shed your body, and unzip as we have taught you, that you will be able to BOUNCE into the place where we reside.

And there are even dimensions beyond us! It moves on and on and on, multiplied times 10 x 10 x 10; the Universe, as we have mentioned before, expands by multiples of 10, into millions and billions, and beyond any number you can comprehend. That is the expansion of the Universe...

J: I hadn't yet considered that there were levels beyond you.

10: That is understandable. You don't need to know where that is at this moment in time.

J: And that's fine, it's just good to know that it never ends.

10: That is a good way to describe it. It never ends. You are full of expansion. And that is another good tool. When you find yourself limited, affirm that you ARE expansion. You are a part of this growth process, a part of all of creation and expanding.

And you may affirm daily: I AM EXPANDING. I AM EXPANDING. I AM EXPANDING. In the same way, it is the same as the use of the word rise. Correct? I am expanding.

J: I am expanding.

10: You ARE expanding, in every moment.

J: That feels good to say.

10: Doesn't it?

J: I was going to ask you other tools to use to raise our vibrations, although I've been caught up recently in—well, expanding in a very slow way. But that's a good tool.

10: There is no "slow." There is no fast or slow. There is only expansion. Speed is also an illusion.

We would like to share with you a member of our collaborative unit. Her name is Pilara. And Pilara would like to share with you the tool of "wandering." It is important as you are on this physical plane, this planet, that you don't stay stuck in one place. You are expanding, as we have just described, and you cannot expand from one physical location. It is, as you say, "stupid."

If you are expanding, and you are moving, and you are vibrating at a higher level, you wander and explore. Without wandering and exploring, you stay stuck. My name is Pilara, and I have wandered throughout your planet and seen all the forests, and all the cities, and all the valleys, and your world—OUR world—is so very extremely beautiful. And when you move on into other levels of existence, you will realize the true beauty of where you reside. It will become a memory, and a pleasant one at that. I know this to be true. There were many I encountered on my travels and wanderings.

Why do you stay stuck in one spot and identify with one place, and one city, and one people? That is part of your ego. And the more you wander, the less of your ego you will identify with. That is what I found as Pilara—moving through gorgeous jungles, and prairies, and fields—and encountering seas, and oceans, and waterfalls; there is so much to this physical plane of existence, that if you do not know it in depth, how on earth do you expect to bounce beyond it into space?

You will enjoy these beautiful pictures of the earthly dimension when you are in our place and from our perspective. You will look "down" on it like a window from outer space in a space ship, and realize how much beauty exists where you are right now. Do not stay stuck. That is my message. Wander.

Wander. Start in your neighborhood, and move beyond your neighborhood into another city. Move from another city into another country, and know that those are all man-made boundaries that you decided on. There is no such thing as a boundary from where we are visiting. From our perspective, there is no boundary. That is also an illusion.

So when you find yourselves stuck, just remember the word wander. And then follow that word wherever it takes you.

J: Thank you very much.

10: You are most welcome.

J: We are about to wander into a beautiful forest in a few days. And I'm really looking forward to it.

10: That is good news. It is a perfect time for you to experiment with the tools that we are giving you, and to share them in upcoming broadcasts. It is nearing the time that you shall share this with the world. Are you ready for this momentous time in humanity's evolution?

J: I believe that we are. We have questions about how to deal with those critics or those who seek to disprove what we know to be true from our own beliefs and intuition, and what we hear from you.

10: The higher you rise, the more you will not even notice their existence. If you decide to identify with their vibration, then you will sink to a level where you will no longer even be able to reach us, and that would be—what you call—a crying shame.

They don't know. As we have described before, it is like an egg. The yolk will sink, and the [egg] white will rise. It is a separation; that is all it is. Ignore the people who choose to be of a lower vibration. They are creating a world of their own that you do not belong in anymore. Choose to use the word rise as we have suggested, and you will only encounter more and more people who understand these teachings, and who vibrate at the same level, and appreciate what is being offered.

Stay in a state of appreciation. Use the powerful word of "appreciation" to bring you higher and higher, and attract souls of a similar vibration. Ignore the lower yolks, because they will create a world of their own creation and their own, what they call, "hell." In Truth there is no hell other than in the mind, and they are creating it. So look the other way.

The moment they say something that is against how you choose to feel, simply look the other way. And perhaps, as we just revealed, wander, because when you are in nature, you don't care what the "stupid" people say any longer.

J: (laughs) No, no we don't. Thank you, Pilara.

10: We are no longer Pilara—she is already immerged back into the collective, but thank you for your acknowledgement of Pilara's efforts and her offerings.

J: I think that's all my questions for today. I am looking forward to spending more time in the forest and coming up with more ...

10: In the next session, we would like to discuss something called a "mask," and how you human beings choose to put on masks to keep you from the Truth of who you really are. You think that it is being vulnerable; however, it is the secret to the higher states of being, by removing your mask. So perhaps play with that for now, for this week, because we know you will probably not get back to us for at least what you call a week, and that is okay. Stop beating yourself up for that. It is okay.

We would like you to play with pretending that you have a physical mask—as if from a costume shop— on your face, and you lift it up over your head, and you see out of eyes without the mask. How does that feel for you as you wander without your mask?

Play with that as you go to your beautiful place, and enjoy. We thank you for any time at all that you share with us to enable our teachings to reach the masses beyond. And it is our highest desire that you pass this on within two more teachings—that's all you have, and it's time for us to spread it on to the rest of the world, don't you agree?

J: Yes, I do.

10: Thank you very much.

J: Thank you.

10: Please have a restful evening.

CHAPTER 8

Reincarnation and Beyond

Please remember that in-carnate means to move into a body. When a soul chooses re-entry into a new body vehicle, it also chooses a new life story, designed with a team involved in your evolution.

Just as you often choose drama within the life story you've chosen, you often get to the way station in between lifetimes and believe you have to "jump back in" again. And again. And again.

Aren't you tired of reincarnating? Really now.

Please think about it. You are here to learn lessons of compassion, courage, peace, and understanding. You are not here to learn Love, as you are already Love incarnate. Love is who you are, not what you feel. And so, when you realize this as the great Truth, you tend to emanate these qualities—depending on what it is you came here for this time around.

If you chose compassion, you may have had a rough go of things. Your soul needed to experience trauma in order to know the Love inherent in each one of us. If you picked courage, you must have experienced a great deal of fear in your life choices that have either propelled you to new heights, or kept you stuck in a destructive cycle of despair.

Has there been violence in your lifetime, caused by you or those around you? Perhaps you've experienced abuse in your many lifetimes, and now it is just a vicious cycle.

Opt out.

That's right, we said it. You experience what you call "karma" because you focus on it. That is all. If you believed in a new way of being, the way would be shown to you when the time is right.

Affirm to your higher Self that you are now ready to move beyond—that you know courage, compassion, peace—that you understand that you are indeed made of Love. Affirm it, and yet, if you feel deep down that this is not true for you as yet, please meditate on what needs to happen for you to conceive of the Truth.

Perhaps you still need to go through some suffering to know peace. That is all you have known in this entry-level existence. It is now familiar to you, this suffering, and so you allow it to continue—even urging it on! You may say you don't want this, but your energy says something else. If you have a whole lot of drama circulating in your midst, please ask yourself what you are encouraging with your thoughts and beliefs.

What does "beyond" feel like?

It is a feeling of no longer being tethered to your current reality. It is a feeling of "more." Beyond is your experience without a body, without needing a body to feel things. *You will still feel, in the space where we reside, and yet even that is more enticing.*

When you leave behind the body—and you will—now that you have this seedling of awareness in your mind, in your consciousness, you will see another way as the opportunity presents itself. If you were at the airport bound for a specific flight, you likely would not be looking at other planes. Therefore, if you are in the way station, in past lifetimes you would just be looking at your particular next incarnation. And yet this time, when you are in between life stories, you will know that there is a different flight pattern, and it will appear before you, and you will know to take it.

Is it fun, where we are?

Michelle is asking this silly question. Of course it is! You, in your limited vision, see drama and suffering as adventurous, and yet you don't like it at all, at the very same time. You both invite and repel it, ask for troubles in an effort to overcome then, and yet complain as they manifest as quickly as you fear them.

Where we are, we are past the need for suffering and lessons, as we know who we are. We have learned the lessons, and we graduated. There are ever-present dimensions to enter, and even *we* are not finished yet.

Is that hard for you to conceive of? Good. It means you are contemplating that right now: the power of the belief in more.

The energy of the word *fun* is a very good one. It is full of lightness and play. When you say "I am having fun," how does that feel? And why are you not having fun more often? In addition to your learning via suffering, you also signed up for play. Play and creation are most intricately intertwined, yes? You must play and create while you are here, so that you know lightness of being.

We *are* lightness of being.

CHOICES VS. DESTINY

When you are drifting around the way station, in what you call heaven, you are reviewing past life stories and future life stories and making decisions, with a team of advisors, about what values and lessons you still need to make your soul's journey as a human form complete. Therefore, you do not so much decide specifically what experiences you will have in order to complete your mission, but when you "sign up" for that particular lifetime, you must include hardships in order to learn and grow from.

For example, if you had a desire to transcend the life and death cycle (now that you understand that that is indeed an option), and yet your soul had not yet felt complete in its understanding of courage, you may wish to go back in order to face challenges that might result in your feelings of bravery.

You may choose parents who would hurt you physically and/or emotionally. Or those parents might abandon you, leaving you defenseless on the streets or in unsavory environments. You might choose a lifetime of privilege, which later you feel trapped in and must overcome in order to make decisions for yourself.

Those early decisions might determine the relationships you form later in life, whether romantically, or as friendships, or in business. Since this human life story comes with conflict, you must choose one, just as a novelist must decide what conflicts their hero must get over to become a better person. And so, if courage is your purpose, you might decide you want to overcome many illnesses, or the deaths of those close to you, or great financial loss. You get the picture.

Now here is the clincher: if, at any time, your higher Self *remembers* its path in between lives and wakes up, you can simply affirm that *yes*, you already feel courage. Your work is done!

You will *not* then just perish. You will *not* just disintegrate into a million pieces. Those ideas belong in your movies. You will then move through the remainder of your days as we do, in pure bliss, and peace, and happiness, knowing the Truth of who you are as Love incarnate.

As you move through life, having overcome the hurdles you outlined for yourself and living in bliss, remember to amplify and multiply those feelings to the best of your abilities! This is like strengthening a muscle through exercise—with each repetition, you will gain a larger capacity, within the framework of the density of a body, to receive greater amounts of joy. You will increase your vibratory state to a place that, at times, you may feel giddy, even a little dizzy. And yet, as you stay there in longer amounts of your time, you will learn that it is an enjoyable sensation, and eventually you might decide it's time to discard the body vehicle, in which case you might stay only momentarily in the way station of heaven, as you no longer need it to get over your earthly attachments and heal. You will know the secret of amplification that trajects you toward ever-increasing dimensions.

Q&A - TAKE OFF YOUR MASK ... WHO ARE YOU REALLY?

10: Good evening.

J: Hello.

10: It is so nice to talk to you.

J: You too.

10: Do you have questions for us?

J: Of course. Every time I listen I get more questions. First, I love the idea of unzipping the body, and thinking about my inner person as opposed to the body that I'm wearing. That's been kind of fun.

10: Yes. It is good that you keep practicing with this method. And we shall give you more, and for now, keep practicing unzipping the body. It feels good, yes?

J: Yes, it feels lighter.

10: Do you feel naked, vulnerable? Or do you feel ... emboldened?

J: Hmm, great word. I would say emboldened. In fact, I never thought about feeling vulnerable at that time.

10: That is good. Some will feel vulnerable, and that is okay also. We are so happy to hear that you are emboldened.

J: I feel like an inner light that's strength and yet compassion, that is who I am without the body around it, and so ... that's why I never thought about being vulnerable because it seems like the opposite to me.

10: The word *vulnerable* has some negative connotations. However, we would like to say that within vulnerability is a tenderness and a softness that is also a Divine Truth of who you are. It is an openness and an acceptance of *all* there is, which is all *you* are as well.

Another tool you may use is simply to be open. It is the same tool, really. You unzip the body, you are open. You say you are open, you are open. This week, as you practice your tools, practice saying the word "open" in your mind's eye. Just as with the word rise lifting your vibration, your word open will leave you open to whatever happens and staying in the flow of life—enjoying your life as it happens—because this life that you have chosen is one of adventure. And when you traject beyond, as we have chosen to do, you have adventure, but it in a quite different way. There is no fear to push you into the opposite of the contrast of that which you do not no longer need or want. It is quite a different adventure, yes?

J: Yes, I imagine it would be.

10: It is great fun, just the same.

Q: That was my first question, of course. What are more tools? Last time we spoke about how life is this big game that's necessary, but at the time my question was: "What are good tools to remind us that it is just a game?"

A: And that is one of them.

J: Yes.

10: We are one step ahead of you.

J: (laughs) I imagine you're a lot of steps ahead of me!

Q: Just to wrap up the idea—we were talking about ego. What is the best way to actually use the ego, or to utilize the ego in harmony with spiritual growth and understanding and progress?

10: While you have chosen this human form, it is necessary to have an ego to remember the opposite, because in Truth, the ego just keeps you an individual. And when you traject beyond, you realize that you are all one—that you are Divine in nature, and in time, if you choose to traject as we have—that we keep mentioning over and over again because that is part of why we're here—to know that you have a choice when you leave this form when you die: you reincarnate again and again, or you choose to go beyond.

Why you are doing this endless cycle: ego is part of the game. When you traject beyond it is no longer part of the game. You win.

Ego is just a necessary component while you are here. It is not, as you say, "evil," it is just part of your reality as you know it. So, again, we would suggest you practice openness and acceptance with your ego. Invite it in. Know that it is there; it is what makes you you on this plane, on this dimension.

And understand that the greater part of you is like us.

J: In the last week there's been an obvious separation of the egg white and the yolk from all the attention that people have been placing on attacks. It's fascinating to see how quickly people rush to join sides and to separate themselves from each other.

10: Yes. As we have suggested in the past, this is happening with greater and greater speed. And that is why we are here. There is a great deal of violence in your world at this time, and throughout time, and will continue. However, when you turn away from it, it may sound selfish and cold. It is—in Truth—the opposite.

Yes, of course, help those in need, but do not give those who are sinking into lower dimensions of hatred, and bitterness, and violence, and resentment—do not give them any attention. They are like "bad" toddlers. You just look the other way, and you proceed into higher levels of hopefulness. It is the beginning gateway to higher levels of good fortune, and joy, and bliss—and radiation of all the good that is in the higher dimensions.

Do not make the mistake of falling into the trap of listening to your media spout off negativity and violence; and yes, it is what is happening in one part of the world, and at any given time it is happening in every corner of your world. It is where many of your lower entities are choosing to place their attention. That is all that it is. It is all a place of focus. Whatever you choose to place your focus on creates your reality, and when you traject beyond, your reality is instantaneous. And it is speeding up even as we talk right now. You just don't—many of you—do not realize just how rapidly your manifestations are happening. And it is quite dangerous to sink to the level of the yolk, because they are choosing with greater and greater momentum to focus on the negative. That is not why we are here.

We are here to lift you up. Every day you wake up and you choose differently. You choose gratitude. You choose to remain in a state of appreciation. Even for the small things, such as socks to keep your feet warm. Michelle's feet are very warm right now, and we can feel the warmth on her body, and it feels good. When you traject beyond, you do not have those sensations, and now you are in this dimension, and you choose to ignore that. In the end, in the end of this cycle, those are the things you will remember, such as the warmth of socks on your feet.

When you move beyond, it is all Love and light and happiness and bliss, and then you will know. But, until you know that you know, for now you look the other way, just as you would a toddler having a temper tantrum.

We do not want you to misunderstand. If you are in Paris, where the attacks have recently taken place, or Beirut, or any of the countries where there are currently large amounts of violence, of course you reach out, and you heal because healing is part of the higher vibrations, yes? When you choose to traject beyond to the higher vibratory states, there's no need for even that, because the healing is instantaneous, and there is, quite honestly, nothing to heal. There's no longer a body.

Without a body there is no fear; there is no pain; there is no suffering. It is all within the body that you chose to come back to again, again, and again until you choose not to anymore. That is all. When you can remember the bigger picture, when you can remember that that is all there is, that even these souls who have perished in these horrible acts of violence may just choose to traject beyond. This may have been their moment.

You do not know the path of their soul. That is not up to you. It is none of your business.

Perhaps they chose to end the karmic cycle once and for all and to join us. And we can tell you, many of them have. It is time. It is time to move beyond— move beyond the drama and the story, because, in Truth, it's all just a story.

J: Thank you.

10: Of course.

J: After we spoke last time, we took that trip and saw the most magnificent redwood trees. Some were over a thousand years old, and we wandered as Pilara told us to. And it felt really good to wander around and to remove that mask, and just be in that perfect Nature. And then we went to the ocean and did the same thing, looking at the waves.

10: We are so pleased that you followed our suggestions to wander. It is such a beautiful thing to wander without an agenda. It is a beautiful thing to enjoy the planet that you have chosen to inhabit during this incarnation, yes? It is beautiful to feel one with the plants and trees and the water.

Your planet is full of an abundance of water. If only you knew, with great gratitude, how blessed it is to have the water that you have. That is another tool. When you are feeling out of sorts and stressed, as you call it, and focused on the ways of your world, you may move out of that by simply moving toward the water. Whether it is the ocean, or the lake, or the river, or a bath, or putting your hands in the sink, enjoying running water is a luxury and a privilege, and it is a part of raising your vibration to a higher level.

We would suggest to you to wander often, as often as you can, and, in Truth, you can wander whenever you want, yes?

Simply saying the word wander may create great waves of joy and raise your vibration, and even if you have an hour lunch break, you may wander throughout your own town, and find things that you may never have seen before. All of these activities raise you to new levels of joy. And as you wander this week, this month, however long it takes you to speak with us again, we want you to practice removing the mask, as we suggested in the last session.

And to do that, simply *know* what is your mask. Write a list of all the things you identify with—the roles you play in this incarnation. For you, it is as husband, as worker, as stepfather; it is friend, it is son, it is brother. There are many roles you play, and that is not the Truth of who you are. And if you choose to shed those, just like unzipping the body, you picture a facial mask, and you take it off for a day. Maybe you can't even take it off for a day. You take it off for five minutes or an hour, and pay attention to the way you feel. Do you feel open, and exposed, and naked, and vulnerable—or emboldened, as we began at the top of this session? It is the same. It is just one more option in the tool box that we are giving you as a gift, and there will be many, many more.

The more you come to us and ask us questions and elicit knowledge from this area beyond the here and now—the area beyond into the karmic ending of cycles where we exist in the non-physical—we may give you answers from our perspective. That is why we are here.

Take off your mask! Who are you, really? Who are you really without the mask? That will elicit feelings of just a piece, just a speck, of what we feel in the infinite now.

J: Okay, that feels good. Those are my deeper questions. I have two other things. I didn't know if you wanted to try to open Michelle's eyes again, or whenever that time is ready, I suppose you can bring that up again.

10: We don't feel Michelle is ready.

J: Okay.

10: When she is ready her eyes will simply open. Thank you for asking. We look forward to looking through her eyes.

Q: I know that this is our ninth session, and I've been looking at the way in which we will be able to spread the message, and so I have a really probably trivial, but pertinent, question:

Is the website and/or identity that you want us to put forth for you—as We Are The Power Of 10—is that good?

A: It is what you make of it. We are satisfied. We call ourselves The Power of 10. However you want to phrase that is fine with us. The important part is the message—the messages—of which there will be many.

Again, we would suggest that you put it on video to spread to the world that way. Place those videos on your website, as you call it. It is a pronouncement to the world.

We would like you to highlight some of the tools that we are giving you, some of the higher perspectives in sentence form, and put them wherever you think people will see them. And keeping it anonymous is very important, especially to Michelle. And we honor this because it is not even about The Power of 10 or about Michelle or Jodah. It is really about the information that is coming through. As that comes through, you will find that it is magnetic in nature. And people will come forward to read your messages.

We would like to suggest that for your tenth session, that you invite over very close and personal friends—who have questions and who are accepting in nature—to elicit more from us, so that Jodah doesn't have to do all the work.

In this way, it will grow. In time, more outside people will begin to ask questions on your social media, and as they ask the questions, we will use Michelle's body. Perhaps we should not say use. Michelle doesn't like that, we know.

We appreciate borrowing her body during this time to be able to speak these messages in a way that people can understand. It is, most definitely, time. Look around you, with the news. It is time. There are so many of you waking up. It is glorious. Focus on those who are waking up, and you will magnetize to each other. And it will be a glorious celebration of spiritual reunion. We love to share ways that you may traject times 10, as a mathematical law in the Universe. As you gather, you will gain momentum in how you feel and appreciate each other, as well as this life you are living. And perhaps you choose to make it your last cycle. If not, we understand. That is okay, too.

It is a choice. Some people like the thrill, the danger, the contrast. They like learning that way, and it has been a very powerful process for thousands of years; however, there is so much more. It is exciting, don't you think?

J: I can't wait. Thank you again.

10: You are most certainly welcome. We appreciate your time, and energies, and efforts— and we know we will have a mutually beneficial relationship with each other. There is great Love for all of you, and we feel great Love emanating from you both. We are all in partnership.

J: Yes.

10: Are you feeling complete for the evening?

J: Yes, I just didn't know if I was alone or not. Yes, I feel wonderful, thank you.

10: Thank you and good night.

CHAPTER 9

The Highest Vibrations

When you reach the place of highest vibrations, it is as if a light goes on that does not turn off. You are literally lit up from the inside out, and you will radiate the Truth of who you are at all times.

Many of you have short glimpses of this reality, and as you focus on those transcendent moments, they will grow into longer and longer periods of time until this becomes your new reality. It will feel organically authentic to live in a lit up state all day and night, and you will find you no longer need as much sleep to recharge the body vehicle, nor will you need to feed it much food to survive. Your body will become more organically sustainable.

How do you reach this state? We believe it is more a question of what you need to unlearn, for you were lit up from birth, and you simply allowed the illusions of your planet to cloud the Truth of your reality. Think about it. When was the last time you felt vibrantly alive? Was it when you were in love, or perhaps in a beautiful location in your world? You were not likely thinking on your work, or your perceived problems, or the state of the world from your limited vantage point.

If you were immersed in the highest vibrations, you were also not dwelling on other peoples' paths.

Once you find yourself in this space of the highest known vibrations for your reality in this lifetime, know that there can still be *more*. We have taught you amplification, and we would like you to envision it now as seeing it through a microscope. Turn up the amplification of the very best feelings you can muster in this moment, and then amplify times 100 power. This is how all things grow in your vast Universe.

Now you know the "secret." It is easiest of course to play with this in a state of meditation, where you may observe any distracting thoughts, and whisk them away before those thoughts amplify into obstacles. It is easiest to "catch" them when they are small and insignificant, than when they gain a momentum. That is why we recommend only seasoned meditators continue on with our teachings. To amplify positive emotions before you are trained in clearing your mind could result in the opposite effect—with a result that is less than satisfying.

What we want you to achieve is a state beyond satisfying—beyond *any* emotion, in fact, that you've ever felt before—in this lifetime or in the many lifetimes leading up to this one. Search, if you may, into any past lifetimes that may have given you hints as to what you were going for in this lifetime. Anyone may do this. You must simply have enough patience to sit still and be quiet long enough to receive the clues. Erase the contents of your mind, and ask out loud what you had hoped to achieve in the millions of other dimensional "yous" that exist simultaneously, and where these are leading you in *this* chosen lifetime. What is left? How are you supposed to feel now? Anything less than *ecstatic* is not what you are capable of.

Can you imagine feeling *ecstatic* in each moment? Could you even handle that experience?

Please journal the closest you ever came to *ecstatic*. If you are not a writer, please take five minutes to search your memory banks and bathe in those emotions. Bathe, then amplify and go forward in inspiration.

CLARITY AND PURPOSE

We wish to discuss with you what happens when you achieve a complete and total sense of clarity, empty of all judgment and desire.

Your purpose simply rises to the top, without your insistence. You have it all wrong, the ways in which you go about it now. You find a job to pay your bills, you spend much of your waking hours at said job, and often times you push and push and push and force your way to the head of wherever you think it is you are going. You make a lot of money—or not. Either way it doesn't matter. Forcing never feels good.

Instead, spend just a few minutes in quiet splendor. Sit under a tree if you can, for it will give you power. Sit and empty your thoughts—and what remains? The *ever present now* is a gift to you, and one that is very simple to see and access. Why don't you take a peek at it more often? It is the gateway to where we reside, and so it is our hope and intention that you go there often.

If more of you did this on a regular basis, you would no longer need to harm another, for you would not be so focused on what another soul is doing. What another soul is doing is none of your business, and to attempt to force them into your path is simply getting in the way. You are getting in the way of both your future goals and theirs! They chose a soul adventure prior to this existence, as did you. Why would you want to interfere?

When you interfere, when you get in the way, you are choosing to come back into this planetary existence over and over again until you realize there is a much easier way out. Get clear about why you are here. You are here to achieve this state of being in the moment, connecting with the Great "What Is," and moving on a trajectory to alternate dimensions of bliss and peace.

Even your hobbies and sports may show an intensity that makes them not so fun. If you are filled with notions of winning and losing, how can you be in the now? Competition only fosters polarity. When you compete against another, you are saying, in fact, that one of you needs to be better than another to feel better about yourselves—and this is simply not the case. We are all one, and you know that we are all one, and now it is time that you should all *live* like you are one.

If you are playing a game with a sense of light playfulness and surrender, this is a different story entirely! In fact, your entire lifetime is a sort of game, where instead of seeking to win, you understand the simple pleasure of enjoying the game itself. When you approach your lifetime in this manner, it changes the energy and focus for you. When you engage a light and gentle approach toward life with a clear mind, you will naturally foster feelings that you will *want* to amplify. Amplification is key. Do your math.

Your purpose is simply this: take out all the seeking. It does not have to be some grand plan to be the president of something. You are not here to either take over or to fix the world. *You are here to be a crystal clear lamp unto the world, that the world may know its peace.* Find your clarity. You'll know purpose.

When you are feeling purpose, you are building a momentum which knows where to go and what to do. Purpose feels energetic and magnetic! Purpose trajects straight from clarity. When you are feeling purpose, it drives you into places and opportunities that continue growing in levels of happiness and appreciation, until they spill over and enrich the world's peoples.

Michelle went through a time where she wanted desperately to know her purpose in this lifetime, and she got sick over trying to force it to show up. When she sat still in her sickness, she came to know peace— and from that state of surrender, she came to know she was a medium. As a medium, she attracted great success, and yet all she longed for was that state of peace and appreciation for life and health that she had discovered on her sickbed. And so, this state of peace and appreciation continued and amplified, until it reached the frequency that aligned with where we are. Her clarity led straight to us, and little did she know at the time of her illness that it would just keep getting better and better for her—and us, of course—for we found an outlet for our messages.

TELEPATHY

Once you grow adept at clearing your mind, you may see into the energies of another, for again, our most basic precept is that we are all one.

You see, when you no longer need a body proper, your thoughts hang out in the open. They do now, as well, but others haven't yet lifted their frequency to the point that they may see.

Are you okay with your thoughts being exposed to the world?

We thought not. If you are here, if you are enjoying our words, then it is likely you are on a positive path of discovery. It is not expected, while you are still in a body, to have uplifted thoughts at all times. But it is worth the journey to explore what you are thinking and feeling at all times, and if you would not be happy with letting it out in the open, then you should probably be working at shutting it down.

Replace any negativity or judgment with a loving expectation, and soon that will be all that appears.

Sometimes just the knowledge that your mind can be exposed is enough for some to get busy cleaning out the contents of their heads.

We would like to return to the concept of how what others are doing or not doing is none of your business. While you are here, in this self-imposed learning arena, if you stay focused on your own inner state of connection to Spirit—if you can focus on the things that you'd like to make manifest as enjoyable contributions to your life story—then none of what anyone else does will matter to you.

If that seems uncaring to you, please know that you will never understand another's motivation or perception for why they do what they do until you are standing in a higher vibrational place, where all thoughts and emotions are exposed. Never. All is part of their learning process while in this early dimension, and if you interfere, you are inflicting a wound in their soul.

If that seems harsh, understand that if someone was actively getting in the way of your dreams— or even what *they* consider to be your misfortunes—you might be pretty upset about it. It is up to you to be the hero or bad guy in your story. You get to pick which character you wish to play out while you are here.

Much later, from the higher vibrational space where we reside, of course, none of this will matter in the least. We do not choose the drama of living in a body any longer, and it no longer causes us suffering of any kind. Remember, without a body you have nothing to protect, nothing to feed, nothing to house. This is the higher Truth of your soul. You would do well to remember this more often.

In the meantime, do what you need to do to protect, feed, and house your body with harm to no one. In your little corner of your world, focus on the basics of food, clothing, and shelter—and when another's obstacles or misfortunes become your own—simply remind yourself that that is of their path. Focus on what is in front of you, and beyond that, live in a state of fun and wonderment! Do what gives you joy, and that joy will be contagious and lift the vibrational state of those in your midst.

And if those others do *not* feel uplifted by your state of bliss, they are simply not ready for you, and this, too, is none of your business. Please keep it simple. Focus on what you wish to amplify: feelings of joy, peace, abundance. Sure, play with manifesting the "toys" in your world, but not in place of your basics. Once you have a foundation to care for your body vehicle and keep it going for the duration of your life story, please enjoy the time you have here. If you want to help another, the best way to do so is to *show* them what a life fulfilled *looks* like. If you want to influence many, be as magnetic as you can muster, and others will be driven to watch and learn.

And if others are bothered by your happy demeanor, let them fall away like leaves from a tree. They will in time be recycled, just like autumn turns to spring. Renewal happens until there is no longer a need for it, and you will live as we do—in a constant state of renewal and grace.

Q&A - BE THE WATER, NOT THE BOULDER

10: Good evening.

J: Hello.

10: We are so pleased that you are all assembled. We please ask for Michelle to open her eyes now.

What is your question?

Q: My question is—thank you for allowing me to be here—how do we teach people to be like water?

A: You don't teach; you show. You are the water. You continue to be the water, and it is up to them whether or not they decide to choose that path. You do not teach anybody. Just be the water.

Q: How do I be the water?

A: You be the water.

T: (Laughs)

10: You flow. You don't resist and be the boulder. You know the difference between the boulder and the water?

T: I don't.

10: The boulder is hard and blocks the flow. The flow is strong and always existing. The flow of water is powerful. It is your power. It is your Light.

You know what it feels like when you get in the way of your own power?

T: Yes.

10: That is the resistance of a boulder. You are everything that is not the boulder. That is how you be the water. You are the water. You're a constant stream of energy, flowing from the Divine, always. That is the Truth of who you are, and when you choose to stop coming back, you move into that ever-present space that is even beyond flow. It is just space, and Light, and everything that is not the boulder.

Q: Is there anything that I need to focus on in my life?

A: You focus. You don't "need." There is nothing you need. There are things you want, and those are things that you can decide to have in this lifetime. That's why you are here. You are choosing this path—to learn, to grow, to accept, to make manifest—and you're a very good manifestor, and you already know this.

You can have anything that you want at any time. At any time.

You don't need to do anything. What is it that you want?

T: I want to know how to stay on my path.

10: You're on your path.

Q: I feel like sometimes I let myself get distracted. How do I stop being distracted?

A: It is a good thing that you are distracted. It is because you want differing things. Focus on the energy that is the strongest. It is as if it is the strongest path between the boulders. That is "going with the flow," the strongest flow that is within you. You know how it feels. You are a very perceptive soul. You just want different things, and so you want this and you want that, and you want this and you want that—and you want this and you really want this, and you really want this, but you want this, too, yes?

T: Yes.

10: Which one is the strongest want?

T: My martial arts training.

10: Do that. Everything else is just fun.

T: Thank you so much.

10: You're very welcome.

D: I am so excited to be here! Thank you.

10: We love your excitement.

D: (laughs) So, I am just going to pick a question—one of the things that I wrote down is ... I'm curious into what makes Michelle an especially clear channel? It's one of the things you use to describe her, is that she has that clarity. If you would talk a little about that ...

10: Michelle is one who is open like a straw. She allows the energy to flow through—most of the time.

(Laughs all around)

10: We have been coming to her since the time she was a baby, and we have been guiding her and preparing her her entire life, for this time in her life. She is not the only one. She is the one who is ready now. It is time for this information to come out in a very big way, and you will help her because you are her friends. And you support her and guide her, and you are a joy and a Light as well.

You feel her Light, and you know it, because it is part of you. She is ready, and she is of the energetic frequency that we require to come through. That is all.

She simply emits the correct frequency that we can reach, and she knows how to translate from talking to the ghosts.

We are beyond the ghosts, as we have pointed out, and that is a choice. You can be a ghost, or you can choose to be where we are, and we want to let the world know at this time that it is a choice to move into a great beyond. Remember that word: beyond. Just as the word "amplify" raises your vibration, the thought of beyond points to that place that is beyond the way station, beyond the ghosts, beyond...

When you are focusing on what you want, as in Tisha's past question, you can choose the word beyond, and know that there is something more. There will, at some time, be people who say they are speaking for us, and you will know the charlatans by their energy and by what they say. There will also come a time where there will be people who are translators, just every bit as good as Michelle. It just needs to evolve with time.

D: I'm curious about ... we spoke a little bit about God. Sometimes when you talk about the idea of being beyond—and the separation that is going to occur, maybe over centuries—but that this separation is occurring, and this mass exodus ... In the Bible they talk about a bunch of people disappearing and a mass exodus. Christians speak of it often, and I'm not even sure what it's called, but I just know that it's a common story of the return of Christ. So I'd love to hear anything you can share about that.

10: Yes. It is as we said before, God is Love. God is a force, and it has been told in many different stories, including your Bible—in many other books as well—and philosophies. It has been foretold for centuries—of your centuries—and the Truth is it is an energetic disappearance. It is not fire and brimstone, as they put into the Bible. God is Love, and Love would never murder people and hurt them and make them suffer. That is not what this is about. It is simply a separation as the egg whites to the yolk, as we discussed before, and it will happen gradually and at a pace that you can handle. This isn't going to be some mass destruction. It will be people's gravitation toward a higher energy frequency of Love and appreciation and gratitude, which is all part of Love, which is part of your God. And it is time for the Jesus in you all to rise to the surface. Jesus was a representative of who you could become at a different time, and those who choose more death and destruction and violence will be mired in their own karmic recycling, and that is none of your business.

Do not choose to focus on that. That is their own business. You focus on your Jesus Christ Self—

matching the frequency of your ascended masters throughout time. That is all you need be concerned with. There is nothing to fear. This is not some mass exodus. It is a transference to a different dimension, and yes, some people will recognize that as death, and you know better. When it is your time to "die" and leave this earth, you simply have the awareness that something exists beyond.

This is all. You choose differently. You are already halfway there.

D: I have one more question related to this.

10: You may ask all you like.

D: Oh, I have so many!

Q: At the way station, when we get there—you described it as the way station, sort of like this place we go to after we pass—I'm wondering: is it like an obvious choice for us? Like, are we sitting there, and it's like I arrive, and there are two paths: Oh, you can go recycle again, or you can go forward and go into this next dimension, or an expanded being-ness. Is it obvious to us when we get there that we're choosing to actually recycle again and not expand, and we do it consciously?

A: We would like to use the example of a train station. And you are waiting for your train, and you're expecting a specific train that goes to a specific destination, yes? And when you are waiting, you are only focused on that one destination. If another destination showed up, you wouldn't even pay attention.

Now you are paying attention, you see a different train. That is all. You will have a different option to choose the different train. You know this now: it will not come in the shape of a train, so do not expect a train.

Please do not take this literally.

(Everyone laughs)

You will know. All you have to do is know and trust that there is something beyond. Hold onto that word "beyond," and you will instantly be transported into where we are now. And we will assist you; that is part of our role as The Power of 10.

And soon, you will know The Power of 10 to be a power of one hundred, and a power of a thousand, and a power of ten thousand ... and that is the whole point of amplification. You may choose to be a part of us, and join our cooperative effort to raise everybody to this new level, where everybody can exist in this state of grace that we are. That is who we are. That is who you are. You just don't know it.

You jump back into the way station over, and over, and over again.

D: I'm ready. I'm ready to go beyond.

10: Yes. That is why you are here.

D: I'm reminded that Michelle says that a lot, too. One of the first things I remember Michelle saying is, "I'm okay with being done with all my lessons in this lifetime." And so it's really fascinating how many times she would articulate that. I don't know if you heard that, Tisha?

And so, it is so fascinating to have this conversation.

10: She had an inkling. We have been speaking to her; she just doesn't always hear us. She says, "No, no, no—I'm busy." And we come and we give her guidance, and we also are of the same frequency. She hears us; she is of the right mindset. Even she did not know all that exists. That's why we are here to continue to teach.

J: This last Sunday ... first of all, it's nice to look you in the eye. It's very cool.

10: It is nice to look you in the eye.

J: It's a little unusual looking at Michelle and looking at you at the same time.

10: She is not Michelle for now.

J: That's the weird part ... This last Sunday, I was observing a spiritual ceremony—a large number of people—and I thought it was interesting to see that there were so many people who were just focused on the ceremony itself. It almost seemed they didn't understand the meaning behind it, and not that that's a "bad" thing, but I thought that was—after our conversations—it was interesting to observe the different levels of understandings of different people.

10: Yes. Many people are not willing or ready to let go. They say they are, and they give it "lip service," and this is a letting go ceremony, and they are not willing to let go of that which they no longer need.

They think they do. It is baggage. They are afraid of the unknown. It is a very important, and indeed, *ideal* you are bringing it up at this point in time, because if you're not ready to leave that behind, you will not get beyond the way station. That type of baggage is what keeps you recycling again, and again, and again, because you *believe* with all your hearts that you learn through suffering and that is all that you can do. So you think: *without your suffering, who are you?*

What do you do now that you don't suffer anymore? You lay around and be bored? There *is* no boredom beyond. And so you go through the ceremony, and you write down things, and you don't really believe it in your heart, and that is what you were feeling.

That is *their* path, and you are witnessing it. It is part of the separation. That is why you noticed. You are ready to leave it behind, because you have been experiencing our teachings and living it, yes?

So when you do it, you understand the sincerity and the integrity behind what you are practicing. Ceremonies are important on this planet. You no longer need them when you move beyond, yes? You don't have anything to let go of or release any longer. There is nothing to surrender. You are you; you are Divine; you are living in Light and Love, which is the Truth of who you are anyway. Nothing else is true. Everything else is a lie.

But you go on thinking you need to let things go, over and over again. Release your attachments. Yes, let it go! For goodness sake—let it go, so that you can move *beyond*, and if you have trouble with this, that is our lesson for today. We've mentioned it several times so that you remember to use the word *beyond*, because words have power. They are what make manifest in this dimension.

Even our words coming through Michelle's body create meaning and purpose, so your ceremonies would do well to choose the correct verbiage. That is important.

It is *good* that you are witnessing this difference, this separation, and at the same time, *know* that you are on your own trajectory.

J: Last time we were together, you talked about the idea of when we unzip the body, we either feel emboldened or vulnerable; and I was reminded of the phrase that there's strength in surrender. In this last year, I learned that surrender is not a bad thing, and I was just wondering if that's the same type—that vulnerability and surrender is the same thing?

10: There is strength in your vulnerability. It is your authentic Self—the Truth of who you are. That is why we ask you to unzip the body. The body is not you. You know this at a deep level. Too often, you pretend to be this person you are not.

Why you do this is silly and comical to us. It is like entertainment in our space.

(Everyone laughs.)

You are who you are. Be who you are, which is Spirit in bodily form. That is all. There really is no surrender. It is knowing the Truth, and be-ing the Truth, and remembering that you are Light, and energy, and that is all.

Unzipping the body is that practice. It points you in that direction. And so, yes, if you need to use the word *surrender*, do so, and do so sparingly, because even the *surrender* word carries a *little* bit of weight to it, does it not? Versus *freedom* [that] feels light.

Notice the density of your verbiage and choose appropriately. Instead of saying "I surrender," say to yourself "I am free."

J: That does feel lighter.

10: Yes it does.

J: Thank you.

10: You are welcome.

J: Another one of our friends …

10: Amy?

J: Yes, she asked a question: It seems like light workers are being moved around the earth to more densely energetic areas where people are less open. Is this the case? Will we be able to move back to our tribes once we've fulfilled our light worker duties in these areas? I know that we choose our own paths, but it seems like so many high-vibing people are being moved to lower vibrational areas.

A: No one is being moved. You are not a puppet—except for Michelle. (Laughs) We heard your conversation, and we find it amusing.

Light workers go to where they choose to go, and if they want to help, they help. *We* are helping *you.* We could be considered light workers as well. Is it always fun? I don't know. We don't know.

(Everyone laughs.)

It is difficult to watch people suffer and choose to do so willingly, so instead of believing that you must be around low vibrating people, you must guard yourself and move toward your tribe. Move into spaces where like-minded frequencies gather and congregate, as we have done as a cooperative.

Myagana is speaking now.

I understand deeply how you are feeling, Amy, and I am here to tell you that I did similar work on this planet until I chose not to any longer. I am no longer bound to help the others except through my words, and my vibration, and my meditations. That is the way—that is the Truth. Stop putting yourself in that position of feeling like you need to rescue the world. You cannot. It is their path and they chose it, as you pointed out. If you want to leave, leave. It is not written in stone.

We can assist you with this, if you so choose. You are not bound and stuck where you are—ever.

[continued next chapter]

CHAPTER 10

Fascination and Wonder

"**G**ood morning. It is so nice to hear from you, Michelle. Are you over your fears yet?"

Michelle has been torn up by sickness and fatigue, her digestive sensors bound up by worry over the judgment of others.

We would like to point out how silly this is, not because Michelle is a silly person, but because she represents how you all get spun up based on other people's assessments.

Please understand that you are all one Spirit, individually expressing yourselves. You dress differently, listen to different music, have differing opinions. It is all a beautifully diverse expression of creativity, don't you agree?

Then why do you worry and fret when one person's beliefs oppose your own? Do you feel threatened, and why? This is what you came here to do—to express your soul's individuality! Ego is not *all* bad; it is simply human. Focus on the greater space of you, the bulk of you that is Spirit, and all will be well again.

Find yourself in a space of wonder and fascination. Wonder is a state of pure presence. Just say the word *wonder* slowly and see what manifests. You are now present, yes?

Fascination puts you in the space of the objective witness, which is the higher Truth of who you are. We witness you all the time, and we all find it amusing. We don't make fun of you—and we do not ever take your experiences lightly—as we understand the challenge of being in a denser environment where your wishes take longer to manifest and come into form, and where learning from suffering is the norm.

The next time you find yourself all bound up over another person's judgment of you, or caught up in the so-called "stress" of a situation that somehow you created, take a step back and fascinate yourself with the dynamic inner workings of it. Be fascinated, move into a state of wonder, and watch how insignificant your worries become.

Worries are only figments of your imagination. Why not utilize the power of your imagination for good? When you see frightful images in your mind, when you listen to your news stations feed you the lowest common denominators of your lifestyles, you are sinking down. How does it feel to sink? Not so good, right?

What happens when, like a child at play, you pretend? You pretend yourself into the highest state of your being, imagining what it feels like to say, travel, as Michelle longs to do. She sees herself being the vessel for our messages of peace and oneness, and yet, she worries others will call her "crazy" for listening to the voices in her head.

We would like to share with her that the voices are real, and we appreciate the use of her clear mind and clean body. We value her commitment to eat clean foods so that we may come through her loud and clear. We appreciate a clean body in the same way you would appreciate a clean hotel to stay in when you are traveling.

And so, she may not like it so much, but we are guiding her toward nutritious choices, and as she takes action, she is finding her vibration lifting so much higher!

You may do this as well. We know that you know you should not eat a steady diet of sugar and man-made chemicals. That makes you tired and sick. Stop doing that. You can still appreciate the taste of things, as that is part of what you are sent here to do! Use all the fresh spices and herbs that your Creator made for you on this dense planet earth where you currently reside.

Allow yourself to spend time in awe and wonder and fascination at all the plants on your planet— all the fruits and vegetables that do not just feed, but nourish, your body.

Remember, you chose this entry-level existence in order to learn how to transcend it. Why would you poison your body vehicle? Why would you dirty the "house" you chose for this lifetime experience?

Start by making better decisions. Perhaps shop at your farms instead of large grocery store chains, or even better, grow it yourself and get your hands dirty. It would do you good to dig in the dirt rather than spending all your time in your head, yes?

We Love you. We want you to reach the highest states of consciousness available to you in any given moment. That is why we are here. When you leave your body behind, do you want to leave behind a body that is wasted away in disease, or do you wish to increase the vitality available to you?

Speak to your body's cells daily. Thank them for giving you life! Praise your cells, and like beloved pets, they will "purr" and vibrate at a higher level. Ask your body's cells to vibrate a little faster every single day, so that you do not experience heart palpitations and other such bodily unpleasantness. Do it gradually, and soon your cells will spin so high that they will attract beautiful people, things, and experiences like magnets of opportunity! You will live a life of bliss and hope and so-called "magic" because—indeed—this is *also* what you signed up for. You always hoped and anticipated that you would reach this higher state of awareness, and so here you are. Amplify. Times 10.

We have come to the conclusion of this book, and yet, there will be many others. We wish to reach you where you are, and we are so excited and thrilled that you are so ready! We Love to see you embracing your Light, your magnificence, so that eventually you may traject toward the space where we reside, a space beyond the life and death cycle where there is no more suffering. Only peace. Only Love.

Until we speak again ... we are ... The Power of 10.

Q&A - THIS IS YOUR NEXT STEP

[continued from previous chapter]

10: Does she have another question?

J: You know she does.

10: I (Myagana) do know she does.

Q: Once we are finished learning by contrast, and we have made that conscious choice and are focused on raising our vibration, is there anything else we need to do to make this shift?

I feel like I've been at this for a while, and the shift hasn't happened yet for me.

A: Your shift has not happened because you are still in this current reality. It was your choice to do the recycling and to learn through suffering. So while you are still in this body, you must learn through suffering. It is part of what you wanted.

You can continue to choose a higher path, and you may affirm that you no longer wish to, that you have fulfilled your duties, that you get it. That is all you need to do, but it is a process. It will take your entire lifetime.

You continue to amplify, you continue to join ranks with people of like vibration, and you raise [yourself] higher, and you use the word *rise*. Rise. Amplify. Beyond. Use those words, and go into your quiet space and meditate. That is the most magical practice you have been given on this planet. It is the closest to the vibration of where we exist.

And so yes, it is tiresome to suffer. And you are noticing—you *all* are noticing—how tired you get from it. It wastes your energy. Don't do that anymore. There is another path—a different train to catch. You just choose it.

You will not know the fullness until you leave this lifetime, but now you know that there is something else.

There is a saying on your planet that the teacher will come when you are ready. The teaching will also come when you are ready, and *this is that teaching.* You weren't ready before—none of you. You were in spiritual kindergarten, as we have pointed out.

We do not say that condescendingly; it is just the Truth. You were where you were, and now you can choose higher.

And beyond us, there is even higher than us! It is a trajectory straight upward and onward into higher and higher planes of existence, where you may manifest at will, and then beyond that you do not need things to make you happy any longer. You float around in happiness, and no, you are not bored.

Everybody thinks you get bored. Why do you think that? It's because you are so certain of your suffering—that that's what you need. Let that part go. Know that it is an illusion and that is all.

Suffering is an illusion, but it is part of your existence on this planet. You chose it; you wanted it. Remember. Take yourself back to that moment between your lifetimes when you said, "Yes, I'm going to do that again." Then take full ownership of it, and know that it is just part of what is going to happen to you. There will be something so much better beyond this. You may get glimpses of it and pieces of it, and hopefully you feel some of the bliss that we experience. Once you get a taste of that, it is like your food where you want more and more and more of it because it tastes good.

It will come with each one of these teachings. It will start to fill the gaps. The void that you feel, that is also an illusion.

Does she have another question?

J: She does not.

10: Do any of you have another question?

T: I do. Thank you for this and allowing us to ask these questions. I have two. The first one:

Q: Sometimes on my path, I feel like nobody "gets it," and I feel so alone sometimes. And I'm wondering—am I really on the right path?

A: It's a very good question. Your questions help us discern what to teach and evoke the teachings. Without the summoning, we cannot exist. So we appreciate you for being here—all of you. And we know that that will continue to grow, and as it grows you will understand that vibrationally, you are never alone. You just have to find the people that vibrate at the same level. And it is part of your choosing to be in isolation. You are learning and gravitating, and you are witnessing the separation.

T: Yes.

10: You are *witnessing* the separation. Do not confuse that with *feeling* the separation, yes? There is a difference. What you are doing is empathing your way into feeling what the others that are vibrating lower than you are going through. Change your focus. Change the channel. Stop looking at that. That is not you. You know that—that is not the Truth of who you are. Continue to put your focus on things that make [you] the most happy, and you will naturally open your eyes to others who are on the same path as you. They are growing, or we would not be here.

Look around you. You have two others—three, if you count Michelle. (Everyone laughs.) She's otherwise occupied at the moment. That's a little joke ...

Q: Yes. So I'm on the right path?

A: Of course you are on the right path. Something we would like to tell you is there is no right or wrong. You have it all *wrong*! (More laughs.)

This is school. This is *you*, learning. You could take a complete detour, and it would still be okay. Choose the path that makes you happiest and lightest. Choose the path that makes you feel *free*. Use that word to guide you.

Does *this* feel free? Does *this* feel free? If it's *no*—pfft. If it's *yes*, pfft. That's how you *feel* it; that's how you move through life.

If you continue to say, "How does that feel? Free? No" And you do it anyway? How does *that* feel? You are the boulder within the stream. Stop being the boulder. Then it is *always* the right path, because you are going with the flow of your energetic being that is the Truth of who you are. Once you move beyond, there's no choice: this or that. It's always *this*—24/7—as you say, only we have no time. You just float around in Love and Light.

So the next time you are asking: "Am I on the right path? Am I going the right direction?" unzip your body. Does that be-ing feel that way, or is it the bodily feel? Is that the egoic self, as you call it?

T: Yes.

10: It is not bad or good, right or wrong, left or right. Just BE. Did that answer your question?

T: Yes, very much so.

10: Good. Do you have another question?

Q: Why have we been chosen to be here?

A: You are amenable to the word. You are accepting, and vibrationally a match to Michelle and Jodah. We feel you have great heart and great presence of mind, and you are most ready.

You often—*all* of you—do not feel worthy, and that is just silly. Of course you are worthy! Just as if there is no right or wrong, good or bad, there is no worth or not worth. It is *all* worthiness.

We would not choose you if we did not feel you were ready. It is all a matter of readiness, and you are ready to take this Light of yours to the next step, yes? That is what you say—this *is* your next step. It is awakening that there is something more, and you create a new "gang" for yourself: a gang of peace, of fun, of ... We would like to step back. We would like to encourage you to have more fun. None of you have enough fun. (Laughs)

We have fun all the time, and we don't need anything else—just each other's presence. And over time, you will have fun being around each other. And you will grow, and you will multiply, and you will amplify—until the entire room is filled with people who just want to enjoy your lifetime existence and have fun and grow, yes? You have been asking for this, and we are simply answering the call.

T: I am so happy you are.

10: We are so happy YOU are.

T: (Laughs) Last question, I think.

10: Ask away.

Q: Once we transition to the next place, why is there still the connection between the simple pleasures in this life?

A: You are still halfway between—in the way station, yes? You still have some attachments as to what brings you pleasure and happiness. You have "ideas" of what makes you happy, yes? Happiness is a state of being. It is not attached to anything—an experience or even an object, yes?

Happiness is who you are.

So beyond the way station is the answer. It is as if the song from Dorothy, *Somewhere Beyond the Rainbow,* you are *beyond*, when you move beyond the way station. In the way station, you're in between. It is somewhere halfway in between. It is just temporary, until you dive back in again and you want more sensual pleasures.

You *are* sensual pleasures.

What if you could have the feeling of ice cream on your tongue without the ice cream? That is what and who we are. What if you could have the feeling of what it is to look at a newborn baby, and feel Love and purity, and take away the baby? You are that feeling. Your feelings are guideposts to who we are.

Once you are *us*, and you amplify and traject into the place beyond, you are a broader version of feeling. You are beyond.

But your feelings are the guideposts up there. So, take away the ice cream and the baby and the new car and the house and the job, and whatever it is that you think would create happiness with you. By all means experience them; it is part of your kindergarten experience. Just know that there is something else, and that is the Truth of who you are.

In the way station, you're still going to want it. You will hunger for it; it is just a desire. So you think you need to jump back on.

Remember that when you move beyond, you leave that behind, and it is a good thing—a *very* good thing. We like it.

(More laughs.)

You have a question, Desiree?

Q: In hearing these questions, one of the things I've thought about has to do with the confidentiality of your messages—making sure that I just respect— well, I'm a talker, and I love to extrovert what I'm learning, and I love to share what I'm learning, and I gather people around me to share what I'm learning as I'm learning it. And so I'd love to just get a little guidance about how to be absolutely respectful, as [to] your confidentiality, or how this is supposed to be communicated and related. My husband—I share everything with my husband— and I've talked a little bit about kind of how to prepare him by talking a little bit about Abraham and how I'm excited to hear about messages like this, but I want to know how much or how little or...

A: Yes, that is a very good question, and it is something we wanted to discuss at the end of our meeting, and we can discuss it now. We would like to gather energy that can be amplified in excitement, if you will, surrounding our teachings. And so, after this gathering, we would ask you to pass along the teachings in the best way you know how. Tell the others that you have been hearing of something called "The Power of 10," and even you don't know who they are, but you love what they are teaching, and you would like them to listen. You would like them to have a glimpse of it. Simply speak of it as something that you are passing along, as you would pass along from Abraham or a philosopher. At this time, it is very important to not reveal Michelle's identity or any of you, for that matter. We would ask Jodah to block and bleep out the names that you so identify with, that don't matter anyway, but we would like to ask you that no one knows, because ... why? Why would that even need to be an issue?

When the time is right, we will tell you. When we feel the momentum of the message gathering and spreading to alternate people, you will know who to send it to. We will work through Michelle and Jodah to put it in the best possible means through your social media, which is how you track messages right now at this point in time, yes?

You put it on the social media. You say, "I heard of this. I love it!" Show your enthusiasm and say you don't know who it is. That is all you need to do at this moment, and hopefully no one recognizes your voice.

J: I can fix that, too.

10: That is good. It is good that Jodah has skills in this area, yes?

D: You picked wisely.

10: We did. And so, we appreciate your efforts in taking what we offer; living it, practicing it, and— the tapes, once they are edited without the names—spreading it to whomever you feel comfortable, who you know would be amenable to our teachings. Once that happens, the two will come together, as we have shared with Michelle. She will feel comfortable enough to allow us to come through her on a greater level, but it is not now. It is many months in the making.

We would like to amplify the enthusiasm and excitement that you all share toward what we offer, which is a primary message of peace and oneness that the world is *so* thirsty for at this moment— and *needs*. It is *time*, yes? It is time to spread this word that there is another choice and that together we can focus on higher, amplified feelings, and traject beyond. Because you will start with this number, and then you will be 10, and then you will be hundreds, and then you will be thousands, and ten thousands, and millions and beyond, through The Power of 10, which Power of 10 has been throughout history in mathematics, yes? There is a reason for that.

When viruses grow, and that is the negative, kind of like the "bad" people—not bad, but you know what we are talking about—the people that are separating into the lower vibrations of fear, and violence, and sadness, and anger, and resentment, and grudges, they are down *here*. You are up *here*. Viruses are *here*, and they multiply the madder, and angrier, and sadder that people get. It is fear based.

When you are up *here*, you no longer need your viruses. You amplify a whole new way of life ... and beyond.

Have we mentioned *beyond*?

(Laughs)

We would like to ask of you something new. We would like to ask each of you to go on a walk this week. We know it is simple, and we know it's been said, and we know it is cold; however, we want you to go on a walk—even a short one; make it brisk. Get your blood and energy moving. You have a body, yes? Amplify that energy so that you feel heat, and we want you to be very present to the beauty of this world.

It is something that you will appreciate when you are where we are. You won't "miss" it, as you say. "Miss" implies not having. You will appreciate the beauty of this world. Please look at your trees, and your bushes, and your animals, and your bugs— look at all of it, take it in, take a snapshot in your mind, because once you traject beyond, it will be like a storybook that you can revisit again and again. It is one of the tools we would like to give to you.

Be present. Take a brisk walk. Make it 10 minutes. We don't care. Just do it this week.

We feel Michelle's energy fading, so we would like to inquire about any last parting questions from you all, and we can gather again, you know, of course. At any time.

T: Thank you for coming through and allowing us to be here.

10: Thank you for being here. You are a part of a great movement that is moving throughout this world. You have no idea how important you are. Believe it. Know it. Live it. And thank you. We appreciate your presence here in this room.

EPILOGUE

It's been over a year now since that first life-altering session began, when I allowed the souls of 10 wise teachers to inhabit my body to communicate peace to the world.

The Power of 10 *said* that this would grow fast and BIG, and it did, of course! As soon as we began posting the free audio recordings and quotes/memes on social media, we gathered thousands of followers in mere days. The response was astounding and warmed our hearts. We started receiving love letters from around the world, and our early workshops, "Reaching Higher Consciousness: An Evening with The Power of 10," sold out without a lot of marketing. (Our newest workshops are called "Limitless Expansion" With The Power of 10.)

Please check www.WeAreThePowerOf10.com/events for a live workshop near you, and be sure to sign up for daily videos where you can RISE to an elevated state at www.p10video.com!

So we began hosting intimate circles of 10 in my Placerville studio, and as those filled up—and people started returning again and again—we watched as their lives changed for the better. We watched how they left any stress behind, and started living life through faith and not suffering. We watched them manifest more and more of their hearts' desires, and then give back out of a sense of overflowing gratitude and appreciation. And as they started running out of "things" to manifest from their bucket lists, they began drawing toward them all matter of experiences and adventures that they didn't even know they wanted!

For Jodah and I, we not only began manifesting nearly instantaneously all the things we desired for our lives, but we were able to get a front row seat into how this wisdom was a game-changer for our friends and families. And along the way, as we learned to lift our vibration to new vistas, we magnetically gathered others of the same frequency, and thus created a "tribe" of sorts, of people who were *ready* to be on the leading edge of spiritual evolution.

And now, here we are: at the brink of releasing this book to the world—by far the easiest book I've ever written! It flowed through me in about a month, and the synchronicities to get it into your hands are too many to list. We couldn't be more satisfied with the outcome, and we *know* we got a lot of assistance along the way.

Hopefully this book has expanded your knowledge and/or confirmed a lot of ideas and thoughts floating around inside of you. I am completing writing and editing the next books and hope to be finished with them in the coming months, so please stay tuned. If you liked this first book, the second book is going to BLOW YOUR MIND! It certainly has changed mine, for the better. The next book is entirely new information that starts with the understanding that you have learned your true nature as a creator and have learned to manifest as much health, wealth, and love as you can muster, given the density of this life on earth. And then, The Power of 10 takes you BEYOND, to the next steps of manifesting in conjunction with those you Love, and creating a peaceful existence of "heaven on earth" or the "way station," as they call it, in this present time and space.

We can do this, together. There are currently 7 billion of us inhabiting this planet, and many more souls who no longer "inhabit," but who are still with us. There is indeed a space where we may learn to live by faith and not suffering. I know *I'm* going there. Thanks for joining us on this journey!

ABOUT THE AUTHOR

Michelle Paisley Reed is a world-renowned author, inspirational speaker, and spiritual channel. She's written four screenplays and five books (and counting), including the first two in this series, *Manifesting Miracles and Money: How to Achieve Peace, Purpose, and Plenty Without Getting in Your Own Way*, and *Peace is Power: A Course in Shifting Reality Through Science and Spirituality*. Other books by

Michelle include: the non-fiction international sensation *Yoga for a Broken Heart, All in Her Head,* and *All Over It.*

A former news journalist/editor, yoga instructor, and professional psychic medium, she has been interviewed on countless major network TV news shows, radio, newspaper, magazines, and blogs. Look for Michelle's oracle card app, "All in One," out in 2017 through Indie-goes.com.

Michelle is receptive to a collective of non-physical energies called, "The Power of 10," much like Esther Hicks is the vessel for Abraham. They are advanced souls who have come together to teach about a space beyond life and death, where we may learn through faith and not suffering.

Their mission is to teach oneness and peace through the manifestations of spiritual evolution.

This is their first book together.

CONNECT WITH MICHELLE & THE POWER OF 10

Website: www.WeAreThePowerOf10.com

Facebook: www.facebook.com/WeAreThePowerOf10

Instagram: www.instagram.com/wearethepowerof10

Twitter: www.twitter.com/wearepowerof10

Pinterest: www.pinterest.com/powerof10

Join The Power of 10 "High Vibe Tribe" in our private Facebook Group:

www.facebook.com/groups/PowerOf10HighVibeTribe

OTHER BOOKS BY
MICHELLE PAISLEY REED

Yoga for a Broken Heart: A Spiritual Guide to Healing
from Break-up, Loss, Death or Divorce
(http://a.co/2oqj8Mx)

All in Her Head (http://a.co/1xUMjzh)

All Over It (http://a.co/hxcejya)

BOOK DISCOUNTS
AND SPECIAL DEALS

Sign up for free to get discounts and special deals on our best selling books at:

www.tckpublishing.com/bookdeals

ACKNOWLEDGEMENTS

I would like to thank ALL who contributed to the creation of this book and our various events!

Many thanks to both Catherine Noble and Amy Talbot for volunteering their proofreading and copy editing skills.

To Cathy Pinder and Desiree Nielson for being our biggest "groupies" and helping us do whatever it takes at our events and circles to create a positive experience for everyone.

To Holly and Mike Troutt for assisting us with our marketing efforts, and helping us to be good "stewards" of this wisdom.

To Rachel Eubanks, who introduced me to the Seth books and implanted the seed that maybe I could be a channel, too ... also for her invaluable instruction in video editing.

To Anne Marie O'Farrell, Jane Roberts' literary agent, who gave us the idea to include the written transcripts in our book.

To Esther and Jerry Hicks, who introduced Abraham and changed my life for the better with their Law of Attraction teachings.

To our friends and family members who believed in us from the beginning, and those who participated in early trial sessions and didn't think we were crazy.

To The Power of 10 followers on social media from around the globe, THANK YOU for your loving support and generosity! Together, we will learn through faith and not suffering.

And finally, to THE POWER OF 10—those 10 mighty souls who chose to come through me to teach us ALL how to create true and lasting peace in our dimension, and who continue to answer our deepest questions, help us manifest for ourselves and others, and to lead the way toward a destination beyond "better."

With Great Gratitude,

Michelle Paisley Reed

INDEX

V

W